Hollywood Royalty

HOLLYWOOD ROYALTY

Hepburn, Davis, Stewart, and Friends at the Dinner Party of the Century

BY

Gregory Speck

Birch Lane Press Book

Published by Carol Publishing Group

A Birch Lane Press Book
Published by Carol Publishing Group
Birch Lane Press is a registered trademark of Carol Communications, Inc.
Editorial Offices: 600 Madison Avenue, New York, N.Y. 10022
Sales and Distribution Offices: 120 Enterprise Avenue, Secaucus, N.J. 07094
In Canada: Canadian Manda Group, P.O. Box 920, Station U, Toronto, Ontario M8Z 5P9
Queries regarding rights and permissions should be addressed to Carol Publishing Group, 600 Madison Avenue, New York, N.Y. 10022

Carol Publishing Group books are available at special discounts for bulk purchases, for sales promotions, fund-raising, or educational purposes. Special editions can be created to specifications. For details, contact Special Sales Department, Carol Publishing Group, 120 Enterprise Avenue, Secaucus, N.J. 07094

A living script of the ultimate dinner party drawn from interviews by the author.

Portions of some interviews have appeared previously in substantially different form.

Photographs are from the private collections of the author and of the guests.

Manufactured in the United States of America
10 9 8 7 6 5 4 3 2 1

Library of Congress Cataloging-in-Publication Data

Speck, Gregory.
   Hollywood royalty : Hepburn, Davis, Stewart and friends at the dinner party of the century / by Gregory Speck.
      p.   cm.
   "A Birch Lane Press book."
   ISBN 1–55972–150–2
   1. Motion pictures—United States—History.   2. Motion picture industry—California—Hollywood (Los Angeles)—History.   3. Motion picture actors and actresses—United States—Interviews.   I. Title.
PN1993.5.U65S64   1992
791.43'028'0922—dc20
[B]   92-1643
                                                                          CIP

*To my mother Nancy, my most faithful supporter,
my most loyal fan, and my best friend,
with love eternal.*

Menu

Hollywood Royalty

OR

Guess Who Came to Dinner

Starring

Katharine Hepburn   Bette Davis   James Stewart
Ava Gardner   Audrey Hepburn   Gregory Peck
Olivia de Havilland   Joan Fontaine
Douglas Fairbanks, Jr.

Costarring

Lillian Gish   Helen Hayes   James Cagney
Loretta Young   Maureen O'Sullivan   Jack Lemmon
Lauren Bacall   Geraldine Fitzgerald   Rossano Brazzi

Featuring

Gina Lollobrigida   Marcello Mastroianni
Robert Stack   Carroll Baker   Rod Steiger
George C. Scott

A Living Script of the Ultimate Dinner Party
Drawn from Interviews by Gregory Speck

Acknowledgments

FOREMOST AMONG THE MANY to whom I owe grateful thanks for the parts they have played in the creation of *Hollywood Royalty* are the twenty-four guests themselves, who granted me the honor and privilege of extended interviews about their remarkable lives and careers. Among them, particular appreciation is owed Katharine Hepburn, James Stewart, Douglas Fairbanks, Jr., and Gregory Peck for their singular efforts in my behalf.

Along the path of my own career, special mention must be made of Andy Warhol, who invited me to write for *Interview*, where my first big pieces were published; Malcolm Forbes, who said that my interviews in that magazine gave it "some much-needed class," and who tried to buy *Interview* in order to make me the editor; Milton Goldman, who told everyone that I was going "straight to the top" and did all he could to assist me in that regard; and Halston, whose words of support and expressions of interest inspired me by their genuineness.

My sincere gratitude is owed to the columnists Liz Smith, Cindy Adams, and Aileen "Suzy" Mehle for reporting my coups and quoting my articles; to the editors Kevin Sessums, Jay Gissen, Kim Blake, Gael Love, Rossella Livraga, Massimo Borgnis, Laurence de Cambronne, Martin Gross, and Nancy Evans for their roles in the publication of my work; to the publicists John Springer, John Strauss, Joel Brokaw, Jonathan Marder, Cynthia Parsons, William Kenly, Cara White, Bill Evans, and William Schelble for their roles in facilitating certain interviews; and to Christian deFrank, Robert Hall, Thomas Kranz, Nadia Spellman, Patricia Wagner, Adele Khoury, James Frasher, James MacArthur, Robert Wolders, Marje Zimmermann, Patricia Scott, Phyllis Wilbourne, James Cushing, Giorgio di Sant'Angelo, David del Valle, Barbara Barondess MacLean, and Lawrence Quirk for their various contributions in putting pieces of the puzzle together.

Special mention must also be made for their exceptional craftsmanship of Steven Brower, Donald Davidson, Arthur Hamparian, and Alvin Marill at Carol Publishing.

Lastly I thank Allan J. Wilson and Steven Schragis for their patronage as the publishers of *Hollywood Royalty*.

Preface

HOLLYWOOD ROYALTY is based upon a series of interviews conducted by the author between 1985 and 1988 with two dozen of the greatest and most enduring movie stars. Each of these one-on-one conversations proved a remarkably open, personal, and in-depth discussion about the life and career of the subject, and most have been published in leading magazines and newspapers, quoted by top columnists, and syndicated globally by *The New York Times*.

In order to incorporate the actual words of a such a pantheon of living legends into a single book, the author returned to the twenty-four transcripts of his conversations with these luminaries and soon realized that, while each of the interviews was individually extraordinary, as a collection they offered an unprecedented perspective on the truth behind the image of those larger-than-life personalities whom we know as "The Hollywood Royals." Sadly, many of them are no longer with us, and indeed several of the participants in this work have recently died, making the contents of the book all the more precious and its publication all the more timely.

Since each interview was written and published as a verbatim conversation in question-and-answer format, and since all of them focused on Hollywood during the Studio Era, it followed that there should be a way to combine all of these intriguing conversations into one extended conversation—at a gathering, perhaps, of the last of the great screen idols, all of whom knew one another, as well as the other great stars, directors, and producers with whom they created cinematic masterpieces.

The result surely represents an entirely new literary form, in which the interlocutor is the only speaker not to appear, even though as author he was the only one present at all of the individual conversations that in compilation form the book. The classical literary antecedent for this presentation would clearly be Plato's *The Symposium*, popularly known as *The Dinner Party*, in which Socrates and his friends express their views on the nature and meaning of Love.

The area of expertise shared by these gifted actors and actresses is obviously the heyday of Hollywood and the beautiful and talented performers who represent it through the legacy of the motion picture. The vignettes and profiles of the twenty-four guests at this event complement, contradict, and amplify each other, whether as character portraits or as revelatory anecdotes, and taken together they produce a total picture from a uniquely "inside" point of view about a chapter of American culture that fascinates all of us.

Thus, the structural organization of the book evolved as a group conversation, in which every word spoken is a true quote from the person to whom it is ascribed. The logical setting for such an airing of memories and opinions was inevitably a grand dinner party, and the ideal place for such an event was of course San Simeon, that legendary California oceanside mountaintop treasure palace built by William Randolph Hearst. It was here that the publishing and producing impresario entertained the Hollywood Royals throughout the twenties, thirties, and forties, and here that he displayed his incomparable collection of antiquities gathered from the far corners of the globe. Cinematically, Hearst himself was immortalized by Orson Welles as *Citizen Kane* in that landmark motion picture, which opens and closes at Xanadu, a thinly disguised pseudonym for San Simeon.

The reader needs only his or her imagination to envision this elegant event, with its star-studded guest list in that most glamorous of filmland shrines. At one end of the long banquet table sits Jimmy Stewart in his tuxedo, flanked on his right by Katharine Hepburn in a lovely gown and on his left by a bejeweled Bette Davis. At the other end of the crystal-and-silver-covered table Gregory Peck holds court between Ava Gardner and Audrey Hepburn. Between the two trios eighteen more legends are enjoying themselves at this ultimate soirée, all of them looking as they did in their prime.

The dinner party begins with cocktails, in which these outspoken and articulate Hollywood Royals tell it all like it was, and like no one else could. Throughout the seven-course dinner party the reader remains a silent observer, perhaps peering through a secret mirror on the wall or even standing nearby as an attentive servant, the classic "fly on the wall" at one of the most extraordinary events in Hollywood history. Not only does this production feature the most distinguished cast ever assembled; it is constructed around the most arresting and absorbing kind of script possible, for nothing beats the truth.

One word of advice for the reader: If ever there was a chance to be there when something fascinating was said, this is it, and so you are urged to listen carefully for the voice of each guest as he or she speaks. If you know these voices, you will hear them, and recognize their familiar accents and inflections, their unique cadences and vernaculars.

Bon appetit!

Hollywood Royalty

SCENE ONE

Cocktails

IT IS ABOUT FOUR O'CLOCK in the afternoon of a beautiful sunny day high above the shimmering Pacific Ocean on the golden California coast. A gentle, fragrant breeze is blowing through the towering palm trees, and birds are singing their love songs in nearby olive groves. We are on the terra-cotta esplanade of a gigantic tiled terrace in front of what resembles an enormous Spanish cathedral. This is none other than the Casa Grande of San Simeon, the legendary mountaintop complex where for thirty years publishing and producing tycoon William Randolph Hearst hosted the most lavish and star-studded house parties in the history of Hollywood entertainment.

This afternoon we are guests at the last and greatest such fête of them all, and although the host is nowhere to be seen, a formally attired staff is already in position to wait upon the personalities invited by Mr. Hearst. As the star-struck waiters move about the huge piazza, offering the guests champagne cocktails served in antique Baccarat crystal goblets from their gleaming sterling trays, those two indomitable queens of the silver screen, Katharine Hepburn and Bette Davis, arrive in their limousines.

The conversation opens with the two outspoken actresses immersed in a discussion about that ultimate artistic medium, film, in which they have achieved immortality. Glamorous veterans Douglas Fairbanks, Jr., and Loretta Young soon join in the recollections about Cary Grant. Jimmy Stewart nibbles on a caviar canapé beside a fountain, then greets Lillian Gish and Helen Hayes as the venerable ladies ascend the stairs. Then Gregory Peck accompanies a radiant Ava Gardner and an ethereal Audrey Hepburn over to the gathering of old friends.

Even the regal sisters Olivia de Havilland and Joan Fontaine exchange insights as the assembled luminaries remember Marlene Dietrich, Alfred Hitchcock, and Grace Kelly. This first course concludes with Gregory Peck revealing his thoughts about a career in politics, for which many thought him suited.

Katharine Hepburn

Well, I just think that film is the greatest medium in existence for attacking any subject you like. Film offers tremendous opportunity for communication, for you can say anything with it. And I was just bloody lucky.

Bette Davis

Well, Miss Hepburn's first part, as John Barrymore's daughter in *A Bill of Divorcement*, was a terrific way to start a film career. She was utterly perfect in that part. Yes, she and I have managed to sustain careers for many years. We came out here at the same time, and both of us had been in the theater. I mean, after all, we arrived here with Jean Harlow and all those gorgeous people. The theater people were very different from the movie people back then. Katharine Hepburn was strikingly different, as was I. The physical thing was not nearly so important in the theater as it was in the movies, for on the stage you are at a distance, and makeup through the magic of the footlights can transform one. The camera, however, does not lie. How you looked offscreen as well was very important.

Katharine Hepburn

I was lucky beyond belief. Of course, I got fired all the time, during rehearsals or after something had opened. But I was seen, and I got the job. I really don't know how people today get in to be seen or to be read. Now you can't get an agent, because first you must join the union. But you can't join the union unless you get a job, which you can't do without an agent, it seems. It was luck.

Bill of Divorcement was a wonderful part for a girl to star in. Then *Christopher Strong* was very glamorous, and *Morning Glory* was a lovely, tricky part, in which I copied to the best of my ability Ruth Gordon, who had been doing a thing called *A Church Mouse*. And then *Little Women*, which is still one of my favorites, was a classic role. So I did those four in one year— 1933—what is known as a great start for anyone. I have known many brilliant actors who didn't become stars. Flashies become stars. Getting the part is very important, too.

What I should be congratulated on is picking the material. But I did make frightful mistakes, too. When you've lived as long as I have you've had a lot of flops, many of which were your own fault. You just have to think, "Now where was I at fault?" But take *Sylvia Scarlett*, which is a classic today. When I did it, in 1935, I thought I was being very funny by dressing up as a boy. Well, I saw it about a year ago, and found it revolting. I have Compton Mackenzie's book somewhere, but I have yet to read it.

I can still recall the first preview, down in San Pedro. The audience was perplexed, and wildly bored, and they began leaving in droves. George Cukor and I were sitting together, and Natasha Paley leaned over and said, "Kate, why don't they laugh?" And I said, "They don't think it's funny." So I went down to the ladies' room, where I found a woman lying on the sofa. I asked her if the picture had had that effect on her, and she just turned away from me. So then I went upstairs and got into my car, which was a convertible, but I guess I stood up too soon, because I hit my head on a metal bar, and thought, "Great, now I'll be knocked out!" Well, we drove back to George's, where we talked with Pandro Berman, who had produced the film. And I said to him, "Don't worry, we'll do another one," and he said, "Oh dear, I'd rather be dead!" It just wasn't any good, but Cary Grant was beyond belief in it. And here I thought *I* had made a mighty attractive boy! Cary was such fun to work with, an actor with lots of energy. I wonder why he stopped working.

Douglas Fairbanks, Jr.

I talked to Cary just a few weeks before he died, for we stayed in touch over the years. I was very devoted to him, and always liked him a great deal. He was an awfully nice guy. I had known him before we made *Gunga Din*, in 1939. We were talking about who would play what role in the film, unable to decide. I suggested that we toss a coin to determine which of us would play which part. That's how we made up our minds. He was always very astute about selecting material, not so much about his own parts, but about the overall picture. He was very shrewd about judging what would be a success. Cary would always choose an inferior part in a film he thought would be a hit over a great part in a film that he thought wouldn't be so popular.

Loretta Young

Talk about professionals! I did only two pictures with Cary, but such a thing as not knowing his lines would never happen. It would never occur to Cary not to know his dialogue. The first film we made together was *Born to Be Bad*; he was so attractive. He just loved games, and his mind was so quick, so agile. I worked with people on my television show who I'm sure never looked at the script before getting to the set. Well, all an actor can sell is his face and his lines, and if he doesn't know his lines he's in trouble.

Cary was an elegant gentleman, always striving for some-

Cary Grant, ca. 1932

thing beyond himself. I think that this is one of the reasons he experimented so extensively with LSD, always under the guidance of a doctor. In those days they did not know that if you took LSD alone you might go out and kill yourself. Cary wrote an article about it, and I think it appeared in *The Saturday Evening Post*. He described the feelings of the medication, or whatever it was, and I remember thinking at the time that I wished he had never written the article. He made it sound so marvelous and appealing it would make everyone want to do it.

Later we appeared together again in a film called *The Bishop's Wife*, with David Niven, in which Cary played an angel. He later said that he had a crush on me, but I don't know if that was simply gallantry on his part or not.

Joan Fontaine

You know, Cary was just about the biggest and most romantic leading man of his day, and indeed to this day. He was very wise about his career, for he made pals with his then agent, Vincent. Agents really were agents in those days. They handled only two or three stars, and they bought properties, and they even read galleys for possible material. Leland Hayward, for example, was one of the greats. He represented Margaret Sullavan, and Henry Fonda, and Jimmy Stewart.

I, too, appeared in *Gunga Din*, but in the making of Alfred Hitchcock's *Suspicion* with Cary I still felt that the leading man had all the power, and I still suffered from the cold shower I had received from Laurence Olivier when we made *Rebecca*. I felt I was there under sufferance, but then they voted me Best Actress that year. Working with Cary was wonderful, but I think that he wanted a departure from all of those light comedies he had been doing, such as *Holiday* and *Bringing Up Baby*, with Katharine Hepburn.

He saw *Suspicion* as his great dramatic role. He did kill me in the original cut, but at the preview the audience objected, so they had to reshoot it. We were told later that the audience simply refused to accept him as the murderer. In the new version, the film just stops, chopped off without an ending. Halfway through the filming Cary realized that the whole picture was being told through the eyes of the woman, which gave him quite a shock, since he had given his approval of my being cast as his wife on the assumption that he would get to kill me. Cary had leading lady approval, which is some power. He was not a casual actor at all.

Audrey Hepburn

Cary was such a cornerstone of the movie industry. He was one of the few absolutely irreplaceable stars. We wouldn't have had all those wonderful movies if someone else had been in them.

I'll never forget the first time I met Cary. Stanley Donen, who directed us in *Charade*, was going to pick me up at my hotel in Paris, and he had Cary Grant with him. The plan was that the three of us could become acquainted over dinner, before shooting began. I was thrilled to death, of course, to be in the backseat of the car with Cary. Well, we got to the restaurant, and the waiter poured the wine, and I threw it right all over Cary. I just knocked it over, since I was so nervous. He had on a lovely pale gray flannel suit, and in my excitement I knocked the dark red wine all over him, ruining the suit. I was mortified, as you might imagine. That is my Cary Grant story. But *Charade* was, I thought, an especially good film, and it had such a wonderful score by Henry Mancini, too.

James Stewart

You know, it was tremendous good fortune for me that Katharine Hepburn owned the play *The Philadelphia Story*, which she had been starring in on Broadway with Joseph Cotten and Van Heflin. In fact, I remember that I couldn't believe that she had me in mind for this great part, as the reporter, in which I would act with two of the greatest stars of the day, Kate and Cary. When I first read the script I thought I was being considered for the part of the fellow who was engaged to her. As I read I thought to myself, "Oooh, that part of the reporter is a good one, but I'll be happy to play the other one." I asked the producer, Joseph L. Mankiewicz, whom he had in mind for the reporter, and he told me that I was to be cast in that role.

I've got to say that Kate couldn't have been better to work with. I don't know where she got that reputation for being difficult and feisty. She knew everything about the play, and George Cukor knew her very well, having worked with her many times before.

Katharine Hepburn

The Philadelphia Story was the film that saved my career. I did it first as a Broadway play in 1939, and then we did the picture in 1940 during a period when I was not doing too well at the box office. In fact, the Independent Theatre Owners had labeled me "box office poison." Doing a play is such a severe punishment for your sins. I learned to stay up until midnight, and then to deliver the next day. Five A.M. is fine for me, but going on at eight P.M. is death.

Anyway, Sam Goldwyn was trying to buy the movie rights to *The Philadelphia Story*, which I owned. I agreed to sell it to him if he could guarantee that Gary Cooper would play C. K. Dexter Haven opposite my Tracy Lord. Well, he couldn't do that. And Jack Warner wanted to buy it for Warner Brothers, which was all right with me, if he could guarantee Errol Flynn would play that part. He couldn't. And then Louis B. Mayer came to talk with me about it for MGM. He was a very shrewd operator, and he brought along Norma Shearer. You see, I had been playing Tracy a full year before I got any offers to make the picture, because they didn't realize that I owned it. So I said to L.B., "Can you get Clark Gable and Spencer Tracy for me?" And he said, "I don't think so, but I will guarantee you Jimmy Stewart, and I will give you a certain amount of money to go out and see whom you can persuade to do it." And so I got Cary Grant.

James Stewart

It was another example of the great good fortune that has followed me all of my life, for I won the Oscar that year, thanks to Kate.

In much the same way that she planned *The Philadelphia Story* as her comeback to the screen after *Bringing Up Baby* and *Holiday*, *Destry Rides Again* was intended as a comeback vehicle for Marlene Dietrich—for she, too, had been labeled "box office poison," if you can believe that, after having made *Blonde Venus* with Cary, and *The Scarlet Empress* and *The Blue Angel*, and *Morocco* with Gary Cooper. Anyway, Marlene was well aware of how important *Destry* was for her movie career, and she realized that she had to top herself if she was to make any more movies after it, so she put all she had into it.

I'll never forget the making of the scene in which she fought with Una Merkel, really like a pair of tigresses. There were a pair of stand-ins for Marlene and Una, and it was amazing how much they resembled the two of them. George Marshall, the director, told Marlene and Una to get started with the scene, and then he planned to have the two stand-ins take over when the actual fighting was to begin. Marlene immediately said, "No, George, we don't need these two girls. Una and I are going to do the fight ourselves, so you can send the girls away." Evidently, this was the first time Una had heard this.

As you know, the fight scene turned out beautifully, primarily because Una got mad at Marlene when she realized that Marlene was really fighting. They were all over the set, just going at it tooth and nail, kicking and slapping and scratching and biting, and it was all Marlene's idea, I remember. When I poured the pitcher of water over them they finally stopped, and the reason that it looked so realistic is that it actually was one hell of a catfight. I believe that it was the best female fight ever filmed. They both got carried away, and especially Una, who had been entirely in favor of having the doubles do the fight for them. The moment she discovered that Marlene wasn't fooling around she began to fight back, and that in turn caused Marlene to pour it on even more.

I liked taking Marlene out to dinner and to dance back in the days of *Destry*, before I went off to war, and so we dated quite a few times, which was fairly romantic. Yes, Marlene was quite a character, but we got so much negative fan mail, since people objected to the idea of a cowboy, especially a sheriff, who refused to use a gun. They claimed that I was distorting the whole tradition of the cowboy in the Old West. In retrospect I realize that *Destry Rides Again* really was a bit of a different slant on all that, but Marlene was just wonderful in it.

Like all the good ones, she was very helpful, too, and she knew the business inside out. There is one thing she said to me that I will never forget. It's really so simple, and you see it all the time, but it's so distracting when you're acting on camera. Not everyone realizes it, but it is very important, and Marlene is the one who told me about it. She said, "Now, if you've got an over-the-shoulder shot, and you're talking to the person, never try to look him or her in both eyes, because you really can't do that. You've got to look at the man or the woman in one eye or the other, without switching your focus back and forth between eyes. Trying to look into both eyes simultaneously is impossible, and it's not only distracting, but also destroys the effect of concentration." She was right, of course. "Now, Jimmy," she said, "we film actors all know that you stage actors play as if you're acting to an audience downstage. So, just keep your eyes focused on my right eye, and the camera will do the rest." It was excellent advice, and I've used it ever since. I often see people trying to look at other people in both eyes, and it just won't work. You can't look someone else straight in both eyes at once, and if you switch from eye to eye you lose the effect.

Years later I worked with Marlene again, in a film called

No Highway in the Sky, about airplane design flaws. We shot that one in London in about 1951. In my opinion Marlene Dietrich made great contributions to the movies, and she was just wonderful to work with, so totally concentrated all the time.

After *Destry Rides Again* Marlene could have anything she wanted out here, and the same thing went for Kate Hepburn after *The Philadelphia Story*. And like Marlene, Kate's a real pro. She came to the set to work, and there was no fooling around.

Rossano Brazzi

That is entirely true. Katharine Hepburn is a fantastic woman —but then, she wants to do everything! When we made *Summertime* together back in 1955 she insisted upon doing that stunt of falling backward into the canal in Venice. David Lean had figured out several ways for her not to have to fall into the canal, but she was adamant, and absolutely refused to use a double. After she went in and came out her eyes were bloodshot, but she said, "Don't worry! Tomorrow I'll take care of it." Well, she still has that condition. That was how she caught the bacteria that to this day causes her eyes to water. We are still very good friends, I am happy to say.

I, too, was really very lucky, after all. After only one test for the remake of *Little Women* with Elizabeth Taylor, I made *Three Coins in the Fountain*, *The Barefoot Contessa* with Ava Gardner, *Summertime* with Katharine Hepburn, and many other films with Joan Crawford, Olivia de Havilland, Joan Fontaine, Shirley MacLaine . . . you name her, all the best. To be an actor, it is often a question of luck.

Douglas Fairbanks, Jr.

I was lucky to work with Katharine Hepburn on *Morning Glory* in 1933, and I've got to say that I adored her, right from the start.

The producers couldn't decide if she would be good for

Marlene Dietrich and Lew Ayres in *Desire Rides Again*, 1930

Douglas Fairbanks, Jr., and Katharine Hepburn, as Romeo and Juliet, *Morning Glory*, 1933

romantic leads at the time, since she had played John Barrymore's daughter in *A Bill of Divorcement* the year before, and she was obviously unusual. She was out of the format of the "glamour girl," and they were a little frightened about what to do with her. So, they put Adolphe Menjou and myself with her in *Morning Glory*, to make sort of a threesome out of it, and of course she won the Oscar that year for it. People have forgotten that the rest of us were in it. Oh, she was, and is, marvelous.

I believe that people have grown to think of her as a beauty, but at the time they didn't. Hers is a kind of beauty that grows on you. I suppose that at the time they did not consider her beautiful since she was so unusual. People began to see her as being beautiful later on in her career. But I've always adored and admired her, and frankly am just mad about her.

Olivia de Havilland

I think that Katharine Hepburn is extraordinary, and I always have thought that. Bette, too, and Garbo especially, for she was the tops. After Greta Garbo I would rank Katharine Hepburn and Bette Davis as the best. They all tried for certain standards and an ideal, and they had a certain originality. Those three I regarded most highly, but I studied the work of lots of others, too, like Barbara Stanwyck, who was quite different from part to part. There were also extraordinary comediennes, like Jean Arthur and Carole Lombard. Irene Dunne was wonderful, too, and I went to see everything she did, many of them with Cary Grant.

Katharine Hepburn

Another part that I loved was *Alice Adams*, with Fred MacMurray as my beau and Fred Stone as my father. What a splendid play about social climbing! You know, one of the great disappointments of my career was that I never heard about it from Booth Tarkington, the author. The play was a very interesting comment on the times, on social climbing without quite enough money or quite enough style. Without anything, really.

In the heart of Connecticut, where I was brought up, they had a place downtown where you walked up a stairway. And facing each staircase it gave the depressing address of the business in the building where poor wretched girls could get a job. And that's how the playwright had ended it. Alice didn't get the man, and I don't think she should have, but in those days in the movies you bloody well got the man, you know. But they wouldn't go for an unhappy ending. I wanted her to climb those stairs, for I think that's the horrible story of everyone's life. It's climbing those steps toward the American Misery, the point at which you decide your dream is not going to come true, and you settle for three meals a day, otherwise known as reality. That was the truth of the American Dream back then. And so we never knew if Booth was disgusted that we put a happy ending onto *Alice Adams*.

Joan Fontaine

I did an enchanting picture called *Quality Street* with Katharine Hepburn in 1937, but under the name of Joan Burfield. It was directed by George Stevens, and it costarred Franchot Tone, and it had lovely clothes by Walter Plunkett. It was just a perfect jewel of a movie, too good to be appreciated, which is why it wasn't successful.

Anyway, I found the name Burfield riding up and down with my mother looking at street signs for a new name. Olivia and my mother felt that we should have different names, so as not to be like the Andrews Sisters, I guess. I wanted to keep the name de Havilland, but they decided to find me a new one. Actually, Fontaine was my stepfather's name. A fortune-teller said it had to have an *e* on the end, so when I suggested Fontaine she said, "That's it! That's a success name!"

My screen debut had been in *No More Ladies* with Joan

Crawford. I was listed as Joan St. John, and in it I was supposed to be her rival for Franchot Tone, who was her real-life husband. It was directed by George Cukor, and I had one line, which I think they cut, but the great designer Adrian made my dress, and it was so sophisticated, since I had the body of a string-bean. I was so nervous back in 1935.

The next year RKO called one morning and said, "You're being previewed today in Glendale. Go over there." So, my mother and sister and I piled into the rented Ford, and sure enough my name was up there in lights, spelled June Fountain, in *Wings of Mercy*. But I would like to have been Joan de Havilland. It's going to be on my tombstone.

At that time, though, Olivia was already a star, having made a number of pictures with Errol Flynn, such as *Captain Blood* and *Robin Hood*. She was at least four years ahead of me. Hell, I guess I was a has-been by the time I was twenty! I made about eighteen B pictures before I became what you could call a first-class star. I received some good reviews for work on the stage, but it wasn't until *Rebecca* that I saw my name up in lights, and all that. I was so lucky to get that part. I had been taken to dinner at Charlie Chaplin's by George Cukor and Paulette Goddard, with whom I had just completed *The Women*. Rudy Vallee, who was always taken with young girls, was seated across from me at the table, and I was next to this owl of a man. We were discussing literature, and I said that I had just read a stunning book by Daphne Du Maurier entitled *Rebecca*. And so he said that he was David O. Selznick, and that he had just bought it the week before, and that I should test for the role of I. de Winter.

Well, I tested and tested, as did Loretta Young and Susan Hayward and Vivien Leigh, until August twentieth, when I married Brian Aherne. Quite frankly, Laurence Olivier wanted his wife Vivien Leigh for the part, and he made it quite clear. Vivien had just finished *Gone With the Wind*, and *Rebecca* would have been a great sequel for her. Naturally, she wanted to work with Larry, too. But she was too beautiful, and she wasn't naive enough. The girl had to be callow, and Vivien was simply too sophisticated.

I still seemed an ingenue, I guess, and I was scared to death by Olivier. In retrospect I must thank him, though, for his attitude helped me subconsciously. His resentment made me feel so dreadfully intimidated that I was believable in my portrayal. I *was* terrified, and I felt unwanted and unloved, and for my twenty-second birthday party during the shooting none of them turned up for my cake on the set. It was the last day, and all the crew had given me little presents. They kept calling for Olivier, Judith Anderson, George Sanders, and Gladys Cooper, and not one of them came. Reginald Denny was crying, and I asked him what the matter was. He told me later that the other stars were all having champagne in Larry's dressing room, and that they couldn't be bothered.

Without Hitchcock on my side it would have been utterly horrible. I was told every day that I was about to be replaced, and I have to say that it helped. As I say, if life hands you a lemon, make lemonade. Well, it turned out to be a nice big pitcher, because I was nominated for the Oscar and became a star overnight.

Alfred Hitchcock was just darling, and a god to me . . . a chummy one at that. Such a dear, sweet man with a wonderfully ribald, childish sense of humor. When I read that he had satyriasis I am appalled. He told me once, "As far as sex goes, I'm so fat that I had to conceive my daughter with a fountain pen!" I've never felt that I should tell this story, but since everyone is so open now, and everyone thinks that he was chasing Kim Novak and Grace Kelly, I will, because none of that was true.

I was with Tippi Hedren once on a CBS show when she said he had propositioned her. Well, what he did was to see her Achilles' heel, and knowing that pretty young actresses wanted to feel that he was a dirty old man, he would play it up. "Yes, I must get into your bloomers, young lady!" he would puff and growl. I can just see him leering at them in jest, but they never realized he was teasing them. It was all a joke. I mean he was only five feet four, and his wife, Alma, a cutter, was less than five feet. They had a very close relationship, and she would pick him up in the car each evening, with their daughter Pat, upon whom they doted.

He had such a puckish sense of humor, and he liked to ridicule people because he felt a very strong class distinction, being a cockney of no background whatsoever, surrounded by all the actors talking about Mayfair all the time. "Oh, I say, how's Binkie Beaumont? And do give my love to Larry and Viv." I'm sure he felt that there was a tremendous clique that excluded him, and so he delighted in tearing them down, though subtly.

Dame May Whitty was working with us once, and Hitch took a champagne cork, which he attached to his fly. So, he just sat there with his legs wide open, with this little cork sticking out, giving her directions. She saw it, but of course pretended not to, and he acted as if nothing was amiss, but we all saw what was happening. That's the sort of juvenile humor and ridicule of hauteur that led people to think he was a wild lecher, when he wasn't at all.

Gregory Peck

If a statue had clay feet Alfred Hitchcock made sure you knew it, and he did like to be sharp with pomposity, in whomever he found it. He *was* that way. He would give it a swat. One quote of his that I like is about how he made the pictures in the office, and how directing the actors was a matter of herding cattle into the corral. He would say anything to be effective with the press.

You got the impression that he hated actors, but that since he needed them he behaved, even though he would have preferred to get along without them. Well, that simply wasn't true. I never saw him demean or mistreat an actor, or even raise his voice. He was absolutely courtly, and kindly, too. Now I know that he was a neurotic man bedeviled by many things, but he was always extremely considerate and kind to the actors. He liked being in the press, being quoted, gaining publicity, and so he made himself good copy, with quotes like that one.

James Stewart

Actually, Alfred Hitchcock would spend at least eight months and even about a year preparing a script before he ever shot a frame. By the time he was ready to film it he knew the picture scene by scene, line by line, moment by moment. Hitch was at the top of the list when it came to that. He was the true master. After he finished one scene and said "Cut!" he would announce to his cameraman, Bob Birch, "The next scene is here." Then he would hold up his hands and make a frame against what he wanted to appear on the screen. Bob would stand behind Hitch and look through his hands, seeing exactly what the director wanted, and then he would set up the camera that way.

I made four pictures with Hitchcock, and I never once saw him look through the lens of a camera. Well, Bob was very fast at setting up his camera the way Hitch wanted, so when he would say to Hitch that he was ready Hitch would say, "Okay, get the actors in here and have them move around a little bit, to see if they're comfortable," which we did, just like cattle in a corral. This is the way he did it, saying to us, "Now technically we're all set here, so this is what you're being paid for, so just go in and see if it works." I think that this is where people got the idea that he looked at actors as cattle. He would have us move about to see if we felt comfortable, and then close it off while we were filming. It was just like herding cattle into a little corral, the way he would have us hustled onto the set.

Of course, before doing a scene the other actors and I would discuss our movements, and decide what we were going to do, to see if Hitch liked it. There was never any of the blocking you get in theatrical rehearsal. He would let you work things out for yourself. If it didn't work, he would give you his own ideas, and generally that would be the key. Every once in a while after shooting a scene Hitch would get out of his chair and come up to me. Then he would very quietly say, "Jim, the scene is tired." He would then go back to his chair and sit down, and you would know exactly what he meant, that the timing and the pace were wrong. But he never took you off into a corner to give you all the motivation and all that.

There is a story about Kim Novak and Hitch that I heard about at the time we were making *Vertigo*, though I wasn't there to see it happen for myself. Kim was actually a substitute for Vera Miles in that picture. Vera was under contract to Hitchcock, but she became pregnant and then couldn't do the part. Kim apparently went up to Hitch when he was sitting in his director's chair in his blue suit and tie, very grandly, and said, "Mr. Hitchcock, I don't really understand in this next scene what my feeling is in relation to Mr. Stewart, and what my motivation is as far as coming in at this particular moment." Hitch looked at her and said, "But Kim, it's only a movie." After that Kim never questioned anything, and was pleasant throughout the shooting.

Doris Day was also a very pleasant person, with a lot of ability and a wonderful voice. It was a part of her talent. I don't think that Hitch had ever done a picture in which people sang, so he was very unsure about that part of it when we made *The Man Who Knew Too Much*. I recall saying to him, "You know, you've got a wonderful singer in the cast, and 'Que Sera, Sera' is a wonderful tune, and I think you should let her sing it." "Oh," he replied, "is it a wonderful tune? I don't know. I don't know about music. I doubt very much whether it will work, but let her sing it anyway."

Gregory Peck

I liked Hitchcock at the same time I knew, even though I might have been a naive country boy, that he was deeply tortured. Anyone who would get to weigh that much! He was huge! He would have to struggle just to get out of a chair. It was some kind of an oral compulsion, I think, with this need for constantly shoving something into his mouth. But you admired him for overcoming it, for not letting it do him in. If anybody in film was an artist it was surely Hitch.

Hitch saw me as kind of rough around the edges, a small-town American boy. I think he liked me, although he wouldn't have been caught dead saying so. It was obvious to all of us who knew him that he had his own inner devils, apart from the big part of his personality that he used in his directing. Anyone who would eat like that has to have some problems.

When we made *Spellbound* with Ingrid Bergman he must have weighed three hundred pounds, and he was constantly nodding off on the set. He would sit in his canvas chair with his four chins drooping, sound asleep while they finished up the lighting. The first assistant, who was very tactful, would stand alongside him and jiggle him to wake him. Hitch would awake immediately and know exactly what was going on. He had the entire picture in his head, in his mind's eye. Every shot and every frame was rolling through his head before he ever started. His whole method of directing was to try to get the movie as close to what he had in his head as he could.

What he saw me as was what I was: a small-town, middle-class American boy, with a few of the rough edges rubbed down. Berkeley had rubbed off on me, and four or five years of doing theater in New York had also. So, he took it upon himself to teach me how to dress. I was given to wearing brown suits, but he pointed me toward gray and dark blue and black. "One wears brown in the country, you know, but gray or navy in the city," he told me one day. Well, I did what he said. But then one day I showed up in a blue suit with brown shoes. They were dark brown, and I thought they looked pretty good. "Oh, Gregory, don't ever wear brown shoes with a blue suit!" he scolded me in his avuncular way.

Then in the matter of wine and food he was also a connoisseur. He and Alma and I would go to dinner at Chasen's, and he was keen on the finer points of what would make a balanced meal. He was very much interested in the food, let's face it, but he wanted to get the proper wine with each course. He did a very wonderful, generous thing, by the way, which he later tossed off. He sent me a case of twelve assorted bottles of wine, each a fine vintage, and on each one he had attached a handwritten label: this is best with roast beef; and this is best with filet of sole; and this is a dessert wine. All of them were Lafite-Rothschild, or Montrachet, or something equally good. Well, I took them home and drank them, and then later realized that if I had had any good sense I would have saved that whole case of wine with the labels personally written out for me by Hitch.

In 1946, you see, I didn't know that books would be written about everything, and that Hitch would become a kind of icon, so I threw them all out! Now they teach college courses in his films, but then I was just trying to make a living. I was damned glad to be working, because two years before that I had been flat broke in New York. I was trying to get my career going, and I wasn't thinking about history.

James Stewart

I think that Hitchcock was one of the true masters of the film business. He wasn't exactly in a class by himself, or better than anyone else, but he had something special, and he was an original, like Frank Capra was an original. C. B. DeMille and John Ford also. Hitch had this wonderful ability to create suspense in the audience, and working with him was always a wonderful experience.

I think that Grace Kelly was simply outstanding in *Rear Window*. God, what a wonderful girl! When you consider that this was only her fifth picture, and that she had already become an absolutely top star, her story is all the more amazing. In fact, it's almost incredible. In filming that movie with her I got the feeling that they were real scenes. She was very, very special.

After *Rear Window* was completed we discussed doing another picture together. It was called *Designing Woman*, and Metro was going to make it, and she said that that would be fine. The costumes for both Grace and myself were all done, and then one day she came into L. B. Mayer's office and said, "Mr. Mayer, I'm sorry, but I can't do this film, because I'm going to get married." "But Grace," Mayer said, "this is fine. We'll have a big reception for you and your husband. Of course you can do the picture!" "No, Mr. Mayer, you don't quite understand," she replied, and then she told him all about Monaco and the kind of life she would be leading as the wife of Prince Rainier.

Personally, I think she made as good a princess as she was an actress. Mayer said that they would get someone else for me, but I said that I wanted to do it with Grace. I ended up not doing the picture, which was dumb of me, because it proved to be a pleasant kind of film. Betty Bacall ended up doing *Designing Woman* with Gregory Peck. I would love to have done it with Betty, but I just backed off from it when Grace pulled out and Greg Peck moved in and that was that.

Ava Gardner

Grace Kelly was a very special woman. She was indeed Her Serene Highness. In fact, she was always sort of a princess, and that's the truth. She was also a great credit to her countries, both of them. The reason that I have a pretty home at all is thanks to a mutual friend of Grace's and mine. His name is George Stacey, and he's an interior decorator. In fact, he did her palace in Monaco.

You know, Grace had handwriting as distinct as her personality. It was distinctively Gracie's handwriting, and it was absolutely marvelous. And George told me that he had received a note from her about a week before the accident, in which the writing was very shaky. In fact, he said that he hardly recognized it. I think, and he feels, that she might have had a slight stroke before the actual accident in the car. But

Grace Kelly, ca. 1957

then certain people just don't die, like Richard Burton, and James Mason. They died in practically the same week, but somehow Richard's death affected me more. I still speak of them as if they're alive. And Grace is the same way.

She was a very special girl, and a wonderful friend, and she had the same face for everything and everybody. There was no "I'm the princess now" attitude at all. She was a great lady, and she was great fun, and she was so cute with a couple of glasses of champagne. Her little nosey would go all red.

She was so sweet, and she never forgot my birthday, all those years after we made *Mogambo* with Clark Gable. It was her birthday first, down there in Africa, and there was nothing in Nairobi except poor lepers on the street. You couldn't buy anything. There was only one lousy hotel, and I mean *lousy*. Actually, we were out in the bush most of the time, living in tents, so that didn't really matter, I guess, but anyway I finally found a scarf for her. And we got a bottle of champagne from some bootlegger, so she and Clark and John Ford and I had a little party out in the tent, for her birthday, and then for mine. No matter where in the world I was after that, each year a birthday present would arrive from Grace. She never forgot, and every year at Christmas a handwritten card, not left for a secretary to do. We were never exactly bosom buddies, but very good friends.

I went to her wedding to Rainier, and to Caroline's—at least her first one—and I visited the Grimaldis in Monaco several times. I also think that Grace gave Monaco a little class, baby. She was such a lady, and a very strong lady, too. I went to have a test at the Princess Grace Hospital in London the other day, and I asked them if it had anything to do with Princess Grace of Monaco. "Yes, she opened it," they said. And now Princess Caroline is the patroness of Grace's wonderful charities. She did a lot of good. She didn't just become a princess and sit there; she was active. She was a wonderful mother, too, as well as a wonderful wife, and he was damned lucky to marry her.

Gregory Peck

We had a house on the Cap Ferrat from about 1966 to 1978 and went there quite a lot in the summer. Of course, I knew Grace Kelly when she was here in Hollywood back in the fifties, and because of our friendship we saw quite a lot of the Grimaldi family during those years. David Niven and Jack Hawkins and Rex Harrison were all there, too, so it was like a film community based around Monaco.

When the kids were little they would go to the palace to play with Grace's kids, Albert and Caroline. Well, one summer day they came home from playing at the palace, and we had a nanny, who was terribly upset. It turned out that my son Anthony had punched Prince Albert in the nose. Anthony was about a year or two older than Albert, and he gave him a bloody nose. I called Grace to say how sorry I was for what Anthony had done to Albert, and she said, "Don't be silly! It was the best thing that ever happened to him! It's the first bloody nose he's ever had, and the first time anyone has ever punched him! Don't give it a thought!" Well, obviously they got off to a great start, and when Albert came to Amherst, Anthony sponsored him and even gave him the nickname "Big Al." I think he liked it, and it kind of helped him to get out from under the burden of being a crown prince, not to mention the son of Grace Kelly.

Lauren Bacall

I didn't know about Jimmy, but I did know that *Designing Woman* had been intended for Grace. She told me later that it had been the one part that had been written with her in mind, and that she was furious that she never got to play it. But, she wanted to be a princess instead. I loved doing that one, for it was a wonderful script with a terrific part.

I had known Greg Peck before making the film, and we'll always be friends, I think. He's just terrific, and he's got a great marriage with Véronique. We've always had good times together. Greg is a very classy man, and I respect him a lot.

Since Reagan made it into The White House it has been a standing joke about Greg running for political office. Since America is so hungry for heroes, it looks to actors for leadership to answer that need. But then I see no reason for an actor not to run for public office. I mean, why not? Why should someone else have more of a right? I don't think that a lot of actors qualify, however.

Gregory Peck

To tell the truth, at one time the Democrats proposed that they would first get me elected to the board of trustees of the University of California, which would serve as a stepping-stone to the governorship of California. This was after Reagan beat Edmund G. "Pat" Brown in about 1964. I had been a supporter of Pat Brown, speaking at rallies and even going on a whistle-stop tour through central California. In every small town where we stopped we would hang out on the observation platform at the end of the train to give our spiel. I liked Pat Brown and thought he was a fine politician, and a fine man as well. So, when he lost he jokingly said on television, "Maybe the Democrats should have nominated Gregory Peck." Well, it was ten years before I heard the end of that, and I was getting calls from London's *Daily Express* and *Paris-Match* and *France-Soir*, not to mention all of the American papers, saying, "Why don't you jump into politics?"

Well, you could say that if my career ever had a peak that was it. I had won the Oscar in 1963 for *To Kill a Mockingbird*, and it was at that time that they must have thought that if Reagan could do it then so could I. I told them all, "No, you've got to be kidding. It's completely out of the question. First of all, I'm just plain not interested. I don't want to do that to my life. I enjoy my life as it is." I said that it was just Pat Brown making jokes, but it persisted, and every time I saw him for the next three years I said, "Thanks a lot for nothing!" Ironically enough I played the President in a film that came out in 1987, *Amazing Grace and Chuck*. Now how's that for a twist of fate?

But I love to travel, and I've got my kids doing interesting things, so why should I mess up my life with politics? If I were going to go into politics I would have done it thirty years ago. But that sort of question kept coming at me, and it's not that I mind thinking or talking about it, but I've never had any ambitions at all to go into politics. It's not that I don't think I could do it well. I don't want to be guilty of excessive humility here, but I like the life I have, and I enjoy my profession. It satisfies me.

But if I ever were to go into politics there would be a list of about six things that I would insist upon first. They would have to be done before I would even accept the nomination. I would name these six requirements, and then the nomination would be out the window. First of all, I would demand that the nuclear arms race be ended, and that we cut way back on armaments production. We would also have to step up our programs for education across the board, but particularly for the disadvantaged. I would probably say that we would have to raise taxes, and that we all would have to pay more of a share to carry out the social programs that all of us know we need. I would want to rebuild the entire infrastructure, for the cities are falling apart. Now right there, that's enough already to defeat me. Anyone who would say such things clearly has no sense of what it takes to be elected, no chance in hell. But I would certainly have a lot to say about the persistent racism in this country, and warn that if we don't move toward a true multiracial society, with total and genuine equal opportunity for all, then the nation will start to fall apart. We cannot go backward; we have to go forward. All of these things would be very unpopular with a lot of people, so I would never be elected. On top of that, I don't want the job.

It's true that I did not have a happy childhood, but I doubt that that had any effect on my politics. I think that this

Gregory Peck, ca. 1947

general leaning toward reform in the area of total equality, regardless of color or racial background, and my concern for the underdog, for the deprived, whether young or old, probably comes out of my years at Berkeley. I was a political ignoramus until I went to Berkeley during the Depression. There a whole tidal wave of new ideas came at me, since before that I had been stuck in La Jolla, which is a backwater by comparison, as was San Diego. Berkeley was a hotbed of ideas about social reform, and a place to express every kind of opinion. I just ate it up. At the same time I was reading and listening to great professors lecture. I took English literature and history and political science, and even psychology and anthropology. Then I became interested in the arts, in the graphic arts and in music, and so it was a great place for me to develop.

I don't know what the hell would have happened to me if I hadn't gone to Berkeley, for I see my life before that time as not going anywhere, actually. I was driving a gas truck, and my parents were divorced. My parents were good people, and it's not that they didn't love me, but they split up when I was very young, and they went in two different directions. I never really lived with either of them, though for three years during high school I did stay with my dad. But he had his own schedule, which was the opposite of mine. I do recall going on vacations with him, which was wonderful. He loved sports, and was a very good father to me, but since he had his own life we saw each other maybe an hour or two daily, or less. So, Berkeley was in every way an awakening for me.

Since it was the Depression, FDR was the first president I was able to vote for, at the age of twenty-one, and those became my politics. I hope that I've been reasonably flexible as time has gone on, but I can see that basically I still believe in an active government, and not less government, though not necessarily more government. But a government that lives up to all its responsibilities to all the people. I can't put it more simply than that.

I would have to say that this country has not fully realized its potential for greatness. We cannot afford to waste the talent, the ingenuity, the imagination, the energy that could be attained with a true multiracial society. The idea of attaining that kind of total equality would seem to me to be the best way to tap that tremendous reservoir of creativity which has for so long been repressed and ignored. It will be a kind of rebirth for the United States, I think. That may sound idealistic, but I believe that you can point to enough examples of people from a minority racial or religious background who, when they finally obtain the opportunity to demonstrate what they can do, surprise everyone. They not only enter the mainstream but also become leaders, whether in arts, science, or business. So, it's a waste, in my view, that we are not giving them all enough opportunity to make that breakthrough, so that they can contribute to American growth, development, and progress.

Holy Christ, I sound like the spokesman for the Great Society, don't I? Just to get off this soapbox I'll tell you another one. It has to do with Lyndon Johnson, when the Arts and Humanities Act was passed, back in 1965, I think. It was when we created the National Endowments for the Arts and the Humanities with federal funding. I was on the Arts Council with a number of fine people, like Leonard Bernstein and Agnes DeMille and Isaac Stern, among others, including the sculptor David Smith. Anyway, LBJ took a surprising interest in the arts all over the nation. The idea was to improve the quality of life in broad terms through the arts, giving more and more people the opportunity to participate. One day LBJ invited me into the Oval Office for a fifteen-minute visit, and he asked me how the Arts Council was doing. I told him what we were doing with the money, and he expressed a very genuine interest in the program. I said to him, "Mr. President, wouldn't it be ironic if, under your auspices, the American Shakespeare were to emerge from one of our theater programs?" Well, he looked at me and said, "Yes, and wouldn't it be even more ironic if the American Shakespeare turned out to be a black man?"

I liked LBJ, and I think it's a bloody tragedy that he got mixed up in Vietnam with a lot of very bad advice from the military and from members of Kennedy's cabinet who stayed on. LBJ didn't understand the situation, but he accepted the advice of the intelligence community, and of the Pentagon, and of McNamara and Bundy and all the rest of them. Then all of a sudden he got his foot caught in a bear trap. I remember him telling me that he knew everything the Vietcong were doing even before they did it, our intelligence was so good back then during the war. "I almost feel sorry for them," he actually said once. He thought that it was all going to be over in six months. But his social programs were excellent, and if he had just had the opportunity to go ahead on the domestic front this country would be quite different today. He would have gone down in history as a great President.

And I don't think it would be a bad thing at all if several generations down the road everyone is *cafe au lait*. Some of the most beautiful women in the world are part white and part black, and maybe a little something else mixed in there as well. This is the way we're going, and if we drag our heels we're going to fall apart. We've got to accept the future gracefully, and to guide it in positive ways.

SCENE TWO

Hors D'Oeuvres

A S THE BELL TOWER CLOCK STRIKES FIVE, the last of the vintage convertibles and Rolls-Royces reaches the summit of the estate, having passed roaming herds of zebras, giraffes, and exotic antelopes collected by Mr. Hearst over the years. The two dozen guests begin to wander about the palatial grounds of this dazzling villa, down a few sets of Portuguese-tiled steps toward a trio of guest houses. Here they peruse the Casa del Mar, the Casa del Monte, and the Casa del Sol, which their host has prepared for their overnight accommodation.

The puffy clouds begin their migration across the brilliant azure sky toward the western horizon, which causes the sun to pop suddenly in and out among the cottony configurations. The breeze has stiffened slightly, but it is still warm as the stars explore the manicured gardens, inevitably strolling down to the magnificent Neptune Pool. One of Mr. Hearst's most remarkable creations, this 345,000-gallon fantasy is dominated by an ancient Greco-Roman temple facade, and flanked by marble colonnades that encircle the turquoise water.

As vivacious Maureen O'Sullivan leads an ever-spry James Cagney around to the left, exquisite Geraldine Fitzgerald finds herself escorted by an attentive Jack Lemmon to the right, while the waiters present a continually changing selection of delicacies to the glittering cast. Voluptuous Carroll Baker pauses to admire an especially graceful sculpture of the Greek nymph Galatea, and debonair Rossano Brazzi finds himself drawn to a 3,500-year-old Egyptian statue of the lion-headed goddess Sekhmet.

The headwaiter occasionally suggests that the host of the party will soon be descending from his library suite in the Casa Grande to join the revelers, but no one seems to notice his absence. They are all immersed in the conversation as it flows from Audrey Hepburn to director William Wyler, and then from Sir Laurence Olivier to studio czar Louis B. Mayer. This second course concludes with an extended appraisal of Greta Garbo, who may have been the greatest of all the Hollywood Royals.

Audrey Hepburn

If it hadn't been for Gregory Peck, just as if it hadn't been for Willie Wyler, my career might have been very different. Greg was a very big star when we made *Roman Holiday*, and he had leading lady approval. He helped to launch me on a career that has brought me nothing but good things and great happiness. I really haven't done that many movies, as you know, but that is for other reasons.

Gregory Peck

We knew that Audrey was going to win the Oscar for her performance in *Roman Holiday* after the first day of work. Willie had her tested in London, and he said to the screen test director, "Just talk to her. Don't play a scene. Just ask her where she came from, and what her life has been up to now." It was a totally improvised test, and she apparently did a lot of funny and charming things. The minute Willie saw it he said, "Don't let that girl get away!" He had a very special gift for recognizing talent.

Audrey walked onto that set never before having played anything but a bit part in a British film. I think she was a cigarette girl in it. Maybe she did a couple of those old-fashioned English musicals with titles like *Salad Days*. They were sort of la-di-da, very 1920s upper class. After a week or two of shooting I called my agent, because my contract stipulated top billing for me. It said "Gregory Peck in *Roman Holiday* . . . Introducing Audrey Hepburn." I called George Chasen from Rome and said, "George, this girl has to have costar billing with me." He was shocked, and said, "What the hell are you talking about? Nobody ever heard of her before!" "They will hear of her," I said. I told him that I thought she was going to win the Oscar for it, too. "I will look like a damned fool if the title billing is left the way it is. This picture's about Audrey Hepburn," I insisted to him. "I'm just holding her while she does her pirouettes!" Finally they agreed to fix it, and of course she won Best Actress.

She had been brought up very carefully, and spoke three or four languages, and yet, for all her breeding and sophistication, she was down to earth. She was just a dream to work with. She's a very funny lady, too, and I have always thought that she should have played more comedy. But again, they seized upon her with this image in mind, and they practically put a halo on her head. In fact, they kept wanting to do the *Roman Holiday* story over and over again. It's not that she hasn't had a great career, or missed much, but I wish that she had been allowed to do a few broad comedies along the way.

Audrey Hepburn

I found out all of this from Willie later on, you see. It was very generous of Greg, I've got to say, and just like him. I could go on and on about him. He more than any other actor was responsible for my career. Of all the wonderful things I saw and did and felt and learned on *Roman Holiday*, I guess the funniest is that I had no idea that film would represent an entirely new chapter in my life and career. All I knew was that I was doing a picture. I had no idea that it would lead to anything else. I was, of course, simply thrilled to be costarring with one of the screen's greatest leading men, Gregory Peck, and to be directed by one of the most accomplished of all

Audrey Hepburn, ca. 1953

directors, William Wyler. Greg was certainly an extraordinary example of professional integrity. He was also very hardworking and disciplined and kind to everyone around him. That is the way one is supposed to behave, so it provided me with the perfect introduction to filmmaking. I started out at the top.

Bette Davis

Willie Wyler was certainly the greatest director with whom I ever worked. Naturally, he knew how to create the perfect atmosphere for *Jezebel*. He was a brilliant director, and I did three pictures with him: *Jezebel*; *The Letter*, in which I played a rather wicked woman opposite Herbert Marshall; and *The Little Foxes*, which Miss Bankhead had done on the stage. All three of them were great pictures, because he was simply sensational. No question about it.

You know, people think that we shot *The Letter* in Malaya, where Mr. Maugham had set it, and that both *Jezebel* and *The Little Foxes* were shot in New Orleans, but all of them were done in Hollywood. We never went off the studio lot for anything back then. All of the marvelous sets were built for us right there. Do you remember that gorgeous opening shot for *The Letter*? You would have thought we had gone to Singapore, but not at all. The back lots could be turned into anything, and the soundstages could be transformed into any-place you could imagine. It isn't so much a question of their not being able to make good movies today; it's a matter of everyone wanting the *real* thing today.

I don't think that going on location helps the process of moviemaking at all. You just sit around and wait for the sun to come out, and that doesn't do anything except make it all more expensive. Reality is not half as effective as properly created sets on soundstages. You can spend millions waiting for the rain to stop. But *Jezebel* was filmed entirely on the Warner back lot, and it won me my second Oscar, playing a Southern belle. I thought that it was a wonderful play, but because of it I turned down Scarlett O'Hara in *Gone With the Wind*. One reason that *Jezebel* was so good was Mr. Wyler.

Olivia de Havilland

Willie Wyler directed me in 1949 in *The Heiress*, which was an adaptation of Henry James' *Washington Square*. Actually, it was at a party one evening at the director Lewis Milestone's that I was urged to go to New York to see a production of *The Heiress* on Broadway. Lewis had seen it, and he told me that he wanted me to promise him that I would go to see this play, saying "That's how strongly I feel about it." I had never worked with him, but something about him was so good, so decent. Milestone was like Max Reinhardt in that way, trying to help me. Such a nice man.

Well, I believed him, so I took the train to New York, and I saw the play, and Milly was right in thinking that I was the one to play the part. I saw it at a matinee, and then I took the train back to Hollywood, where I decided what to do, since I had to choose the director. There were three possibilities: Anatole Litvak, George Cukor, and William Wyler. Well, I went with Willie, and we did it for Paramount, and I won my second Oscar for it.

I would say that *The Heiress* is among my best performances. *The Snake Pit* also. You know, both Ralph Richardson and Montgomery Clift were so complicated to work with on *The Heiress*. Monty was very talented, and he cared a lot about his work, and that's worth respecting. He was working at that time with a young Polish girl, a very talented person whom he had met in the East. She was his dialogue director. He would come onto the set with a very fixed idea of the scene as she had worked it out for him, for which she would play Catherine, my part. This was sort of distracting, because at the end of every scene he would look up to see what she thought. She would be in the back, and they had some kind of signal system, and if she would signal negatively then he would ask to do the scene again. Now that was something of a trial for me, and it proved a great cloud to Willie, too, to await her verdict as to whether the scene had gone all right for him.

Ralph was kind of difficult, but all right. There were ways to relate that to the scenes I did with him, for he played my difficult father. He had just been knighted, so Willie was very impressed with him, for he had a title, and he was British. Actually, I was British, too, but I didn't have a title, though my great uncle did. It was a higher title than Ralph's, too, but Willie didn't know that. I'm not sure I knew it at the time either. It didn't matter that Ralph was difficult, for he gave a brilliant performance, and that's all that counts.

Audrey Hepburn

Willie had enormous patience, with us as well as with himself. There are stories about how he would insist upon thirty or forty takes of a single scene until he thought it was right, and then he would not know which to choose.

He was always terribly patient with me. When we got to the last scene in *Roman Holiday* we were in the car, and I was saying goodbye to Greg. Not being a professional actress at that point, I couldn't cry when I was supposed to. The tears were simply not coming while I was sitting in the car, about to be driven away from him, but I did not want them to have to put the artificial tears on my face; that seemed all wrong, too. It was getting very late at night, and everyone on the set was at the end of his nerves and exhausted. Then, after being so gentle with me, Willie simply blew his top. He got so angry at me! "What do you think you're doing? You're not professional at all! Do you want to stay here all night?" he shouted at me. So, I burst into tears, and he shot the scene, and that was the end of it. Then he gave me a big hug. He was so angry, but he knew that one way or another he had to get to me for those tears, and he was right.

I loved Willie, but then all of the directors I had—from Willie, Billy Wilder, and King Vidor to George Cukor, Blake Edwards, and Stanley Donen—were quite wonderful. I mean,

by starting out with Greg Peck and Willie Wyler I thought
that all actors and all directors were going to be like that. I
know that others have had different experiences, for people
can behave in very different ways, given different situations
and in the company of different people, but I truly liked all of
those with whom I worked. Willie directed me again, too, in
The Children's Hour, which we made with Shirley MacLaine.

Shirley and I together made movie history, I think, or at
least created a record. We were the only actresses ever to be
sent off a movie set for giggling. John Huston had once gotten
very put out with Lillian Gish and me for giggling on the set of
The Unforgiven, but Willie actually threw us off the set. I
believe that I was going up the stairs, and Shirley was coming
down, and something happened. Perhaps I said something the
wrong way; I don't recall what set us off. It was a very serious
scene, too, but we simply could not get past one another
without collapsing in fits of giggling. We just burst into
laughter. Do you know how painful it can be to try to hold in
laughter that wants to come out? We kept shooting the scene,
but each time we would have to stop, so finally Willie sent
both of us home, severely reprimanded. The next day we
returned and behaved as we were supposed to.

Gregory Peck

It was just after we finished shooting *Roman Holiday* that
Willie and I went up to London. Two things about that trip
stick in my memory: one was Willie Wyler's fiftieth birthday
party in a penthouse on top of Claridge's, which was the
apartment of Alexander Korda, who was a regal man of immense charm, very Hungarian. I still recall his toast to Willie,
in which he said, "Now that you've reached the age of fifty,
my dear boy, don't expect any more surprises!" I was about
thirty-five at the time, and I thought to myself, "God, fifty
will be the end of the line!" I remember being very upset.
These Hungarians, like the Kordas, have a way of being
totally convincing with that overlay of *savoir faire* when what

Vivien Leigh and Laurence Olivier, *That Hamilton Woman*, 1941

they're saying is an absolute crock, as I found out when I reached fifty. There were lots of surprises left for me still! More and more surprises come along, the older you get—but then, nothing really changes.

The other thing I remember about that visit to England was seeing Olivier in this fourteenth-century abbey that he owned in the country. I can't recall the name of it, but it was something like Norwood Abbey, or Norwich Abbey. He was very proud of it, and he had done a beautiful job of redoing it. I recall that Wyler, Olivier, Vivien Leigh, and I all went for a walk through the fields and the woods before returning to this grand and very comfortable home he had bought. It was cold outside, but very warm inside, and of course he was at the height of his fame, just flying through the clouds, for everything he touched turned to magic. He had done *Oedipus* on Broadway, and he and Vivien together had done the twin bills of Shaw's *Caesar and Cleopatra* and Shakespeare's *Antony and Cleopatra*. They were really the most glamorous couple in the world. I was just awestruck.

Olivier had such great respect for Wyler that he treated him as a schoolboy would treat a schoolmaster. This was because Willie had taught Larry the art of screen acting, when they did *Wuthering Heights*, I guess. When Olivier started to make his move from stage to screen he apparently was all over the place, resounding with his pear-shaped tones, and making grand gestures for the people in the balcony. Wyler was very blunt about it, and said to him, "Now what the hell do you think you're doing? The people aren't fifty yards away! The camera's right here, Larry! We can all see and hear you very well, so don't *act* the part, *think* the part!" Olivier was always grateful for this kind of directorial advice, and he paid almost constant tribute to Wyler in his book. As far as acting went, Wyler was Olivier's guru.

Lauren Bacall

I got to know the Oliviers just before Bogey and I took off for Africa to film *The African Queen* with Katie Hepburn and

John Huston. Danny Kaye and his wife gave a big party for them in L.A., and we had an instant friendship. We all got along very well, and we remained friends.

I adored Vivien. She was very complicated, but terrific. She was truly a lovely woman: beautiful, talented, smart, just divine. It was at the home of the Oliviers one night in London that I met T. S. Eliot. One is, of course, always somewhat in awe of those people, people who write that well. He looked kind of like a professor. He was in a wheelchair that evening, too, as I remember, but I'm not sure if it was an affliction of his limbs or what.

Katharine Hepburn

I was there when Larry Olivier brought Vivien out to test for *Gone With the Wind*. In fact, I stood for her at their wedding in Santa Barbara, while my friend Garson Kanin stood for Larry.

Olivia de Havilland

Vivien Leigh was so charming, and she had that inner strength, that will which Bette Davis also has, but in a different form. She didn't suggest physical frailty, but I suppose she was.

She was deeply in love with Larry Olivier, too, and she suffered a lot because he left for New York to do *No Time for Comedy* with Katharine Cornell, right at the time Vivien was shooting *Gone With the Wind*. She must have been desperately unhappy, and he must have missed her as well during the run of the play on Broadway, and during the shooting of the film. So, one Saturday he got on the plane and flew out to Los Angeles to see her for about four hours, then got back on the plane to fly back to New York. But he missed the curtain Monday, held up by a storm somewhere along the way. Of course, Miss Cornell was not pleased, for she, too, was a tremendous professional and hated to let down the audience. To her it was a serious breach of professional conduct, so she made Larry promise that he would never do that again. I am told, however, that they did meet once again in Kansas City.

George C. Scott

Laurence Olivier was one of the finest actors with whom I ever worked. We did *The Power and the Glory* for television, and we became friends forever. I admired him enormously.

Once at four-thirty in the morning Olivier and I were sitting there at the NBC studios years ago in Brooklyn, and he's next to me, exhausted and hurting, crying with those damned lenses in his eyes, and he's not well. But he was such a class act, so tough and such a survivor. There's not any question that Laurence Olivier was one of the finest people I've ever known, apart from being a great actor.

Rod Steiger

In my view Olivier's most fantastic performance was simply getting through *King Lear*, at his age and in such ill health. His performance was another matter altogether, though, and it was utterly brilliant, but the fact that he was able to do it at all was unbelievable.

Gregory Peck

It must have been about '78 or so that Larry and I did *The Boys from Brazil*, and we had a wonderful time as Mengele and Wiesenthal. We went to the Vienna Opera together, and Larry had a dinner one night at the Hotel Sacher for Véronique and myself with Lilli Palmer and her husband. I will never forget the evening we walked into the Vienna Staatsoper, where there were lots of titled folk in attendance, wearing lots of decorations and heavy jewelry. Larry had been laughing and joking and making rude noises in the car, but the minute he stepped out in front of the theater all the counts and the no-accounts and all the rest of them were wiped out.

He was simply the most royal and the most regal of them all.
He was not to the manor born, but he could do it better than
any of them, knowing exactly what he was doing the whole
time.

We had great fun making that picture, although we really
had only one scene together, the big one at the end, when we
were fighting like animals. We were rolling around on the
floor gouging and scratching and kicking with the Doberman
pinschers about to claw through the door. Of course, it was all
choreographed. We would do three or four gouges and a kick,
and then stop for a while. Then we'd do a punch and a scratch
across the face with a quick knee in the groin before taking
another break. In between takes we would lie on the floor and
chat, trying to keep from laughing, for it was after all a scene
in which two old men really wanted to kill each other with
their bare hands.

Then when the dogs come in they have their fangs bared.
All the snarling and vicious barking and growling was added
later on, you see, since these dogs were really pussycats. I
mean they're not going to put Laurence Olivier, let alone
Gregory Peck, in there with a bunch of killer Dobermans.
They were the sweetest dogs you ever met. When they were
lunging they were simply retrieving something to take back to
the trainer. It could be your sleeve or the shoulder of your coat
or your arm, and you would wear a leather puttee underneath
the sleeve. This goes even to the point of retrieving the knot
on your tie, for when they jumped at my throat they were
actually trying to take my tie back to the trainer standing
behind the camera. It could be your pant leg or anything, and
the dogs are sitting there with expressions that seem to say,
"What can we do next? What do you want us to do?" All the
snarling was done in postproduction. Just before each take the
trainer would say "Fetch!" When it's all cut together it looks
like they're tearing me to pieces. It took three or four days to
film that scene, you realize, and most of the time Larry and I
were lying around on the floor.

And then, much more recently, in about 1985, I was one

of the producers of the Oscar show, and we had the bright idea of asking Larry to come out and present the Best Picture award. Well, out he came, with his manager, Larry Evans, and Mrs. Evans, and we put them all up in bungalows in the Beverly Hills Hotel. We had a rehearsal on Sunday afternoon, and all Larry had to do was to walk to center stage, about halfway forward. We told him that he would probably receive a huge ovation, for which he should be prepared. He knew how to acknowledge an ovation, so we advised him to deal with it as he wished, and then to walk to the podium on the left, where he would find a card with the five nominees listed on it. Furthermore, there would be an electronic prompt board out in the audience with all the information on it as well in lighted letters. He was to read off the five nominees, and in the rehearsal he did it perfectly, with dummy names. He sat out in the auditorium for a while, enjoying some of the goings-on, and then off he went.

He was "home free" that day, but the next night it was a bit different, with millions of people watching. There were three or four of us who put the show together, and we were backstage watching it all through a monitor. After three hours of anxiety, but no major glitches, and nothing too terrible, Larry walked out, and the ovation was like nothing I had ever heard. They went bonkers. He was staggered, and I thought he was going to pancake right there on live television. He apparently lost his bearings, too, perhaps for the first time ever, and went right over to the podium and picked up the envelope. I turned and said to Larry Gelbart, one of the producers, as well as the writer of the show, "My God, I hope he's not going to announce the winner without reading the list of nominees!" But we couldn't see what he was doing.

Then, all of a sudden, he booms out, "And the winner is *Amadeus!*" All we could think about was *The Killing Fields* and *A Passage to India*, wondering if he had been looking at the prompter and was simply calling the first of the alphabet-ically listed nominees the winner. We froze, and then it struck us that this was possibly the biggest mistake in the history of the Academy Awards, an historic mistake made on live television by the man many regarded as the greatest actor of them all.

But by this time the producer of *Amadeus* had run to accept his Oscar, and then he and Larry both disappeared. The closing titles were already on. I first went to Larry's dressing room, and the first one I saw was F. Murray Abraham, someone whom Larry, as far as I knew, had never even heard of before. Well, "Salieri" had beat me to Larry, and I heard him boom out, "Sir Laurence, have you seen *Amadeus?*" Larry had no idea who Abraham was, and he said, "No, no, old chap, I haven't seen it." Abraham looked crestfallen, then rebounded with "Well, see it, Sir Laurence; it's a good picture!"

When we got Abraham out, I asked Larry, "Did you read that title off of the prompter or off of the card that was on the podium?" He looked at me and said, "Well, I haven't the slightest idea." That didn't help any, so we sent someone out there to see if the card was still on the Lucite podium. It wasn't, so we tried not to imagine the consequences if the real winner had been another picture. Then it occurred to us that Price Waterhouse certainly would know, but we couldn't find them either. They had already climbed into a limousine and taken off for the Beverly Hilton Hotel, which is forty minutes away. There was nothing to do but to follow them, so all the way out there Larry Gelbart, Bob Wise, and I and our wives were improvising a press announcement, trying to figure out how to inform everyone that *The Killing Fields* had really won the Oscar. Or maybe it was really *A Passage to India*, since we just didn't know. When we finally got there we spotted these guys and grabbed them by the lapels and breathlessly demanded "The real winner?! The real winner?!" They replied that it was *Amadeus*, so you can imagine the relief. For about forty minutes we were on the verge of coronaries, and to this day I don't know for sure if Olivier got the name from the card or from the prompter.

As for acting, I recently read Larry's book on acting,

which I liked a lot. I did not like his autobiography, by the way, and thought he should have skipped it. The acting book, though, is a great work for people of the theater. It's full of practical information, as well as insights into how he's tackled the great roles, how he found the inner spirit, the character, and the emotions of those great parts, how he went about creating an exterior that revealed the interior. The gospel of acting is "Whatever works works," I suppose, and this book does an excellent job of demonstrating that philosophy.

Geraldine Fitzgerald

I worked with Larry Olivier a couple of times, first in *Wuthering Heights* and much later again on *The Moon and Sixpence*, which was about Gauguin. He was always lovely to work with, just a marvelous man. I saw him in *Oedipus the King*, too, and I must say that that and Orson Welles' *Julius Caesar* take precedent in my mind as being the two greatest theatrical events I have seen.

Larry played it as a contemporary story, which is something that he and Orson shared, I suppose. It gave the story a timeless quality, and Larry was incredibly handsome in it. He looked like a man you see on one of those Greek vases. He played the King as so conceited, so sure of himself, even as all the cattle were dying, and all the people and mystic figures were coming to plead with him to right the wrongs. Slowly you see him begin to realize that there is some connection between himself occupying the throne and the famine and plagues afflicting the land.

When it is all spelled out for him that he has murdered his father and married his mother, that he was the young man who long ago killed an old man on a road, you see a smile break onto his face, as if he appreciates the horrific irony of fate. And only Larry could have done it like that. Then you see a profound change in his face, as if a conscience is born in him for the first time. He let out a little kind of sound, and

Geraldine Fitzgerald, *Wuthering Heights*, 1939

you could feel the audience begin to panic, for they couldn't tell what might happen next, though you could feel that something absolutely ghastly was about to take place.

It was like a faint falsetto "oooooh" that filled the theatre. He didn't go mad, nor did the audience, though they thought they might. Most people will tell you that the screams were when he went inside and put his eyes out, but that is not right. Anyone who saw it can confirm for you that instead of loud piercing shrieks, he let out only this faint little noise, and it was that that made you feel you were going to go mad. A loud yell would have released the tension, but Larry instead decided to hold it. After he had put his eyes out he returned to view, with the blood streaming down his cheeks, and one hand on the shoulder of each of his two daughter/sisters, who lead him away, and that was the end. It was quite a catharsis. I have to say it was the greatest thing I ever saw.

Maureen O'Sullivan

Although I made *Pride and Prejudice* with Larry Olivier and Greer Garson, I had no scenes with Olivier in the picture. The funny thing about the film is that when it came out it got bad reviews. It wasn't looked upon as being very much of anything, and now it's regarded as a classic. Everyone had wanted George Cukor to direct it, but we ended up getting Bob Leonard, who was considered kind of a "commercial" director. The film looks much better now than it did then, I think. Time lends a certain patina to some things, and it ruins others.

Anyway, I saw Larry Olivier when I was in London, and he agreed with me that *Pride and Prejudice* had seemed such a "nothing" film. I became great friends with Greer, and still am to this day. She has been ill, and the last time I called her there was no answer. She invited me to her ranch in Texas, but for some reason I couldn't go. I must say that she is a clever, witty, erudite lady, and I like that in people.

Gregory Peck

Greer Garson had already won the Oscar for *Mrs. Miniver*, another one directed by Willie Wyler, by the time she worked with me on *The Valley of Decision* in 1945. My recollections of Greer are totally unlike L. B. Mayer's, and I guess the general public's. I thought that she was really a comedienne. She's Irish, too, you know, from the north of Ireland, and she can be very funny. She can clown with the best of them. But L. B. put her into that slot, a typical mistake, as the noble-minded, self-sacrificing housewife and great lady. He gave her picture after picture with that kind of character to play.

But I saw her quite differently, as a redheaded Irish girl with a lot of pluck, with lots of clownishness. I still call her "Big Red." She married a wonderful fellow with a lot of money named Buddy Fogelson, and they live in Dallas. They also have a great big ranch in Texas. She comes to town now and then, and since he has thoroughbreds they can very often be seen at the track. I've always loved her, too. L. B. Mayer thought that he had corralled a grand English lady. Well, she *is* a grand English lady, but she's also a very funny redheaded Irish girl.

Katharine Hepburn

Since I never had an agent or a lawyer I always dealt with Louis B. Mayer personally. His lawyer always went over my contracts, and I would say, "Now, Mr. Mayer, you wouldn't cheat me, would you?" He was a very nice man, with a romantic attitude toward the movie business. He was fascinated by it all, just as I was.

And when I made that speech against censorship during the McCarthy era I was severely censured. I had just finished making a picture called *Song of Love*, which was enormously hurt by my making that speech. So, L. B. called me into his office, and demanded to know why I had made that speech. And I said, "Mr. Mayer, you would have told me not to make that speech, and I would have made it anyway, and then we would not have been friends, so it was better for me not to tell you about it. Now I think that you have a right, as the head of this studio, to quietly let me go. And if you do, no one will ever know why." And then he said, "That's not what I'm talking about. Why did you make that speech?" And it kept going in circles, but he didn't remove my salary, or do anything.

I made that speech because I felt I could afford to be fired, for there was nothing in my background that could be attacked, such as religious belief, or foreign citizenship, or membership in any organization. So, there I was: the person who should make the speech.

James Stewart

I have always disapproved of the stuff that has been written about the so-called moguls, L. B. Mayer and Jack Warner and Harry Cohn. Writers usually claim that these men were in absolute control of everything, and that talking to them was like talking to an actual mogul. Well, to me they seemed as far away from that as you could get. Most of the long statements and books about these men, their individual characters, the quality of their work as producers, and how they related to their actors and directors are completely wrong. I just don't agree at all with the ugly things said and written about these movie impresarios. In fact, most of my friends in the industry disagree with that point of view. These men simply did not fit the descriptions given them by people these days, and in fact, most of the people writing these books never came close to knowing any of them.

First, each of them had a complete love for the business of show business. Second, all of them had tremendous good taste. Third, none of them was afraid to take a chance, by which I mean that if one kind of film proved successful they wouldn't turn out six more with the same formula, as they do today, calling them sequels, as with *Star Trek* and *Rocky*.

They had no interest in sequels. They wanted variety, and they wanted to use the motion picture screen as a *visual* medium. The spoken word is the key to the art of the stage, but the visual image is the key to the art of film. Television is a combination of the two forms, taking from both while improving upon neither. The studios were responsible for the development of film art as it evolved and was perfected.

As an example of how important variety was to the big studios, let me recall one day on the lot at MGM. On one soundstage they were filming a movie starring the Three Stooges, who in fact had been supporting players for comedian Ted Healy, when he was in vaudeville. On the next set they were shooting one of the *Andy Hardy* pictures with Mickey Rooney, while just beyond that one they were doing one of those great big musicals. And just past that soundstage they were making *Romeo and Juliet*. Now it's pretty difficult to come up with four more different kinds of movies, and yet all of them were being produced simultaneously at Metro.

This was the kind of variety that Mayer reached for in his desire to create movie entertainment. He felt that the audiences deserved variety, and that it would be wrong to keep showing them the same story over and over again, as they do today with all of these sequels of *Star Wars* and *Rambo*. At MGM in those days you could look at the schedule over weeks and months and even years, and you would find everything from *The Wizard of Oz* to *Ben-Hur*. These men weren't afraid to try anything, especially Sam Goldwyn. He would take risks. He and people like him were really responsible for setting up the motion picture business on a firm foundation. They built Hollywood into something positive that lasted for many years. It's something quite different today.

Loretta Young

We used to crab about how L. B. Mayer and Sam Goldwyn would boss their stars around, but stars needed it, and they still do. Those moguls knew what they were doing, because stars need a lot of attention. They need being taken care of, and encouragement, and discipline, for they are in a business where they are making their livelihood by making faces and showing their emotions. That is not average. In order to be that wide open, you need someone there to fend off the people who want to get to you to see for themselves in person what you're like. Otherwise, you would never be able to act.

Maureen O'Sullivan

I knew L. B. Mayer, but only slightly. Actually, I liked him, though I've heard that he pulled things on many people. He sent for me once, and when I got the message I thought to myself, "Oh, God, what have I done?" No one in my family had ever been remotely connected with the theater, so when my father wrote to Mayer he sent it to "Dear Mr. MGM." He informed Mayer that his daughter was not writing home frequently enough. So, when I walked in the door of Mayer's office, he told me to sit down. "You're not writing home often enough, young lady!" he announced very sternly. I said that it was probably true, and then he countered with "You are not a good daughter!" He was really giving me hell, and then he showed me a picture of his own two daughters. "Now look at these girls. They're different from you. They write their parents, because they care. Now you be sure you write your parents every week from now on." He saw himself as the father of everyone under contract in his studio. I was really very fond of him.

Then, when he left the studio much later I was with him at dinner one night. I had had a number of children by John Farrow by that point, and Mayer said to me that he never felt that my marriage would amount to anything. "Ah, all these children. It's wonderful!" he went on. He was very sweet. I'm glad that I'm not alone in my opinion of Mayer. He did what he had to do, and he was honest, and he was a very nice man, too. He was genuinely concerned about the welfare of his stars. I can remember seeing him coming at me on the lot, looking like a little duck with a bunch of chickens following him in a line. They were his producers.

James Stewart

I can recall my first meeting with Mayer. It was on the set of *Murder Man*, my first picture, which was starring Spencer Tracy. I had only a small part in it, but Mayer came around to the set. Actually, he went to all of the sets perhaps three times a week to make sure that everything was going smoothly. I remember that he went over to talk to Tracy for a while, and then I was introduced to him.

Once I was offered the chance to play a part in a film being made by another studio, so my agent took me up to see L. B. in his office. He refused to loan me out that time, and only once when I was offered a role by another studio did he loan me out. One always had the sense of a powerful hierarchy at work in the studio system, with Mayer on the top and then the big producers and directors directly under him.

Also very important and influential was the publicity department. They were the busiest and most constructive of all the departments when it came to developing an individual career, particularly when you were just getting started. They kept you at work all the time, whether it was in the gym, trying to put a few pounds on me, or on the road, promoting a new film.

Ava Gardner

Metro *never* wanted me around, you know. The idea was "Toss her out, and loan her out, and give her away!" They got well paid for giving me to the other studios, but I didn't. I was in slavery for seventeen years. I started off thinking I was making $50 a week, but it turned out to be $35. My sister and I got to Hollywood in 1941, and for the first three weeks I wasn't even paid. I had a seven-year contract *on their part*, but

Ava Gardner, ca. 1958

they could have sent me home with nothing after three weeks if they had wanted.

I of course had no lawyer, no agent, nobody to help me, and I knew nothing about contracts. Twelve weeks into the year I was put on layoff, so my $50 income became $35, and we had no money to live on. Anyway, Mayer loaned me out all the time, and never took very much interest in me. I can't say that I blame him very much. I think that they just didn't take me seriously at all.

Very few of my films were made at Metro. Toward the end a few of them were.* In *East Side, West Side* I was supposed to play the lead, but then they got Barbara Stanwyck, who was a much bigger name at the time, and so they moved me into the smaller role, which was a much better part. I never had any scenes with Stanwyck, who, I'm afraid, is still on the box every week in reruns. I hear that these old stars on new soaps get very difficult, but I don't really know. Anyway, they just switched roles on me. Metro was always treating me like that, but that time it worked to my advantage.

Gregory Peck

When I first got to Hollywood I went around and met every-body, among them Louis B. Mayer, who did his crying rou-tine for me, because I refused to sign an exclusive contract with MGM. He gave me an Academy Award performance, with real tears dribbling right off the end of his chin, but I said to him, "Mr. Mayer, I would love to work for you, but I'm a stage actor, and I want to continue to do plays as well as movies. I want to work for you, but I can't sign a seven-year contract." He wanted me to join his family of stars, the biggest in Hollywood.

When I left there I told Leland Hayward, my agent, "My God, Alfred Lunt couldn't have given a better performance."

---

* In actuality, of Ava Gardner's first twenty-three movies, all but five were made at Metro.

"Oh, he does that every day," Leland said to me. "That was nothing." Leland had seen it a dozen times before.

Douglas Fairbanks, Jr.

Everyone had problems with L. B. Mayer, as far as I can figure out. He threatened everyone with ruination if he or she didn't do exactly as he said. He tried in many cases, and in John Gilbert's case he succeeded in ruining a very important career. He tried also to ruin Bill Powell and Myrna Loy and a few others, but he didn't quite succeed with them.

Greta Garbo often said that she thought that Mayer was trying to ruin her career, but I don't really know. Probably her decision to stop after *Two-Faced Woman* was due to trouble she had in dealing with Mayer. I worked for him once indirectly, and he was pretty rough stuff, let me tell you. I knew him socially, too, but he was always very nice in those situations. I had gone to kindergarten with his daughters, by the way, Irene and Anita, but my relationship with him was pretty remote.

Lillian Gish

Everyone at MGM knew that Greta Garbo was having an affair with Jack Gilbert, and that she was just playing with him. Well, as a result her popularity went right up, so Mr. Mayer called me into his office and said to me, "You are sitting way up there on a pedestal, and nobody cares. Let me knock you off, and everybody will care." I didn't know what he was talking about, so I said, "Well, what do you mean, Mr. Mayer?" He said, "Let me arrange a scandal for you." You see, I had never had any sex thing in my life. Mother wasn't there, for I guess she was off with my sister Dorothy someplace in England at the time, and I had no one to talk it over with.

Well, I realized that I had to give a performance onscreen and well as one offscreen, and I knew that I didn't have enough vitality to do both. So, I told Mr. Mayer, "But this will mean a performance as a sexpot offscreen as well as my work onscreen!" Without knowing it, I was "the unattainable." So, there was more sex gossip about me than about Greta Garbo, who *was* attainable. I just was not a sexpot, and never have been. Anyway, Mr. Mayer tried to arrange a sex scandal for me, and I said, "No, I don't want one." Then he said, "You know, I can ruin you." "I know you can, Mr. Mayer," I replied. Then he sent word out that if anybody ran a picture of mine or used me in any way he would never be in the movies again. That's the kind of man he was, and the kind of power he had as the head of MGM.

I heard about this, and left the movies to go back to the theater, where I had started. The first thing I did was Chekhov's *Uncle Vanya*, and for six years I enjoyed great success in the theater, on Broadway and elsewhere. This was in the thirties. After that I went back to make some more movies.

But in the twenties I was working twelve hours a day. When they asked me if I wanted to remain unattainable I replied with a question: "What kind of wife would I be?" All of my energy went into making pictures, and since the unions didn't even exist until after the twenties there was nothing to stop producers or directors from having us work at least twelve hours every day. "I'm just dead tired when I get home, and I would make a terrible wife. I couldn't take care of a husband, and I wouldn't want to ruin a man's life," I said to Mayer. Thank goodness I never did marry a man. My life was an open book. They knew what I was doing every minute of every day and night. They controlled me when I was making films, and then when I went back to the theater I had one success after another, in *Uncle Vanya* in 1930, in *Camille* in 1932, in *The Joyous Season* in 1934, in *The Old Maid* in 1936, and in *Hamlet* that same year.

But as for Garbo, she came from a country where they had sunlight three months of the year, and the rest of the time it's pretty dark. They are all very dour people as a result, I think. They are all "inward." I went to Sweden in the summer once and looked up at night, and there sat the sun. It didn't move. The rest of the year there is almost no sun. I think that's why Greta Garbo was always so reclusive. She, like most Swedes, was very inwardly directed. They are an "inside" people. But after working twelve hours a day in front of lights and cameras, who wants to go out and have a social life? It drains you of energy.

Bette Davis

I don't know anything about Miss Garbo except that I have worshipped her for all these years. She was a tremendously talented personality. She was probably the greatest exponent of the art of working in front of a camera. I don't think that there was ever a move she made for a camera that wasn't absolute poetry. She was simply wondrous.

Katharine Hepburn

She and I both made a number of films with George Cukor, but I knew her only well enough to say, "How do you do?" What a tragic shame that she stopped making pictures!

Bette Davis

She couldn't have made the same films, censor-wise. She could never have played the *femme fatale* in the forties that she did so brilliantly in the twenties and even in the thirties. Mae West was another one who suffered from the censorship of the Hays Office. She couldn't do those risqué parts any longer. It certainly was a shame, too. No more visions of Garbo in *Flesh and the Devil*, and no more scenes of Mae West doing her thing in *I'm No Angel*.

Actually, the salvation of Garbo's career is due to a man named Harry Ettinger. As long as the movies were silent she was all right, for she was not expected to give any interviews. But when the talkies came out people wanted to hear what the stars had to say. Well, Garbo and the silence bit was a stroke of brilliance. Garbo was not good at giving interviews in the beginning, for she said things that were just ridiculous. She simply was not very bright about that kind of thing, you see, so he came up with the idea that saved her career: "I want to be alone." It was truly a brilliant idea, a terrific gimmick. There is no question about that. Not only did it save her from being expected to give interviews, as every other star did; it made her seem even more remote and divine and mysterious.

Do you remember the film *Anna Christie*, when you had to wait fifteen minutes to hear her voice? That was her first talkie, you see, and no one had ever heard her speak, so the suspense was doubled. You can imagine what a sensation she made when at last she spoke. What a brilliant idea it was!

You see, so often the voices of those gorgeous people simply didn't match their looks. John Gilbert is one of the best examples of that. Jack's career was over as soon as his voice was recorded for the talkies, even though he had been a very big star of the silents. He had a very high, rather nasal little voice. That was it, or it would have been, but Garbo and he had been having an affair, so she let him do things with her, like *Queen Christina*, trying to save his career. It didn't work at all, however, so he quickly faded from the movies in the early thirties. But Miss Garbo's voice was just exactly as you hoped it would be: soft and sweet and sexy, the most beautiful "Anna Christie" voice! Oh, it was wonderful!

Douglas Fairbanks, Jr.

In 1928 I made *A Woman of Affairs* with Greta Garbo. That picture was taken from a novel called *The Green Hat*. MGM had bought it, and then decided that to get around the problems they would change the title and have one of the characters, whom I played, die of drink, instead of dying of syphilis. Since it was during the age of Prohibition they could never show the bottle with a label on it, so you had to guess whether it was gin or whiskey or whatever inside this bottle. It proved to be a very successful movie for both Garbo and John Gilbert, just as it had been a successful play before that.

Greta Garbo was simply a dream to work with, and very easy to get along with. She was terribly nice. But she would never give an interview, and shunned all that kind of attention. I think she was happy with her life the way it was. She didn't give a damn about what people thought of her, whether they loved her or thought she was crazy. She lived the life she wanted, for if she didn't she would have moved back to Sweden permanently. She liked to move around where people didn't recognize her. She led a quiet life, with a group of friends, and she sometimes took off for a weekend to Europe or the Caribbean. Her friends protected her, knowing that she really was an honest-to-God private person.

She was always conscientious about her work in the twenties and thirties, but then when she had had enough of it, that was it. I think that she was wise to stop when she did, right at the top of her career. My father used to say jokingly that people, when they reached the top, should be shot, so that they could be remembered at their best. He used to tell his friend John Barrymore that he should have been shot after *Hamlet*, rather than letting himself run down as he did. There really may be something to stopping when you're ahead, as Greta Garbo did.

Back in those days, in the twenties and thirties, she did lead a social life—within limits, of course. Most of her friends were part of the European set, like Emil Jannings, for instance. She liked the Continentals and the Eastern Europeans best, I think, as well as the Germans. I remember that on occasion she would ask me to go with her to one of these parties, and I wouldn't understand a word. I would just sit in the corner while everyone else would chat away in German or Swedish or Hungarian or Polish or Russian—I was never sure what language it was. Then when she was closely tied to Gilbert I didn't see her at all.

But I have to say that she was just lovely to work with. I suppose in retrospect I would have to say that Garbo was the greatest actress with whom I ever worked, but at the time I didn't realize it.

Maureen O'Sullivan

I made *Anna Karenina* in 1934 with Greta Garbo. I'm not sure I ever saw that film. I've been told that it's one of her best, but I was always working so hard I never had time to see the films I was making. I did get to know Garbo pretty well, though.

The first time I ever saw her was when we were shooting the ballroom scene in *Anna Karenina*. I had always heard that she was badly dressed and rather slovenly. When she breezed into the room she was wearing an English cashmere sweater the same color as her hair, and I thought she was absolutely gorgeous, with her hair up and in slacks. She was very natural, casually walking over to talk to Bill Daniels, the cameraman, and the rest of the crew. She took great interest in how they were lighting the set, and she was so nice about it all. She had the dressing room next to mine, and they had built a garden around hers to keep people out. I suppose that that was how she wanted it, even though she was basically very friendly and nice to everyone.

Her love affair always seemed to be with the camera, rather than with the person sharing the screen with her, whether it was Fredric March, or Clark Gable, or Robert Taylor, or Ramon Novarro, or Charles Boyer. When I had my one longish scene with her I didn't get anything back from her, and I wondered how it was going to look on the screen. When I saw the rushes I realized that all the magic was there, and that the camera picked it up, for she was having a love affair with the camera. I expect it's been that way with a lot of people.

She really wasn't at all reclusive back then, for she would make jokes—lousy ones, to be sure. She had a rather childish sense of humor, but I liked her. One day when the filming was over I was walking toward her, and there was no way I could avoid her without being rude, since she was coming toward

Greta Garbo, *Mata Hari*, 1932

Greta Garbo, *Anna Karenina*, 1935

me. When we got close to each other I thought to myself, "Now what do I do?" for I had been told that she didn't like to talk to people when she was finished with a project. So, I turned my head as if I was looking at something else, to spare her conversing with me, and she said, "And now vat is de matter vit you?" I replied rather sheepishly, "Well, I was told that you don't like for people to speak to you after a film is over." She looked shocked and said, "*Vat* people? Dat is *terrible!*" I never had any contact with her after that, and I'm rather sorry about it, too, for she was very nice, and I really did like her a lot.

I suppose that she really was the greatest film actress of them all. Certainly to work with her you didn't see anything so extraordinary, but on film she was incomparable. People talk about how Mayer tried to destroy her career after *Two-Faced Woman*, but I firmly believe that it was a self-imposed retirement, and very much her own choice. She was only thirty-six, you know, and she probably wasn't too ambitious. If she had been ambitious she would have gone on like Bette Davis and Katharine Hepburn. I really shouldn't speak for her, since I don't know for sure, but I think she simply was not that ambitious about her career. I don't think she cared that much about acting. In any case, I feel that at the age of thirty-six you really don't have to retire, especially if you're as gorgeous as she was. I mean she could have done anything she wanted, on the stage or on the screen. I just hoped she had enough money, and I suppose she did.

James Stewart

In 1935 Henry Fonda and I shared a house in Brentwood not far from one occupied by Greta Garbo. I met her, but I never really knew her, and like everyone else I was a complete "fall-down" for her. During her career, and even today, she was looked upon with awe, which I think is justified, for she was something so special, and perhaps the very greatest of them all. I don't believe that anyone holds against her her well-known opposition to publicity, and in the end it worked in her interest, I'd say.

I once did something that truly solidified the fact that I would never have a date with her. I was just enthralled every time I saw her. On the MGM lot she had a room, or a bungalow, up away from everyone else, and that was way back in the thirties, when I was just starting out. She also had a limousine that would take her from her bungalow to the stage where she was filming, possibly *Camille* or *Conquest*, and it was no more than twenty yards from her dressing room. She never walked those twenty yards in either direction. The limousine would take her to and from the stage, so she would never have to see or speak to anyone except on the soundstage. She was never seen in the commissary, either. Well, I just wanted so badly to see her up close in person that I thought I would bust. I never expected to be allowed to say hello to her, but I just wanted to see her in the flesh, since she was so utterly captivating on the screen.

Well, once I was making a picture on a soundstage right next to where she was filming her picture. I knew the sound man up on the boom where she was shooting, so one morning I saw him before she got there, and I said to him, "Anytime you see that you're finished please let me know so I can come over here and have a look at Greta Garbo." He agreed to do that for me, and I knew right where to go, because I had seen where she had her driver park the limousine, and I knew that there was only one way from the stage to the car. It was a very easy matter for me to get from the stage where I was working and walk down a corridor to her stage.

Well, it didn't happen for a couple of weeks, but then one day I got a call from my friend on the boom. It was about five in the afternoon, and my friend said to me, "She's just finished and will be heading out to her car shortly." I was not working at that moment, so I hurried off down the hallway and turned the corner, where the door to her soundstage was open. Well, I raced through it, and as I did so I ran into someone, whom I knocked right down on the floor. There was

Garbo, flat on her back at my feet. I had knocked her down on her ass. I wasn't quick enough, either, for before I could do or say anything she was halfway up on her feet. "Couldn't I help you?" I asked, as she said flatly, "No, you can't." Then she headed straight for her car and drove away.

Twenty years later I met her at a party, and I said to her, "I've always regretted something that happened a long time ago, and I've always wanted to apologize to you for it." Well, she looked right at me and interrupted me, saying, "I know exactly what you're talking about: you knocked me down!" She didn't want to hear anything about it or accept my apology, and that was the end of it.

Joan Fontaine

I, too, knew Greta Garbo, and she was so charming and amusing. We had dinner together in Paris and New York. She really was the most delightful, feminine creature, but because her last two films, *Ninotchka* and *Two-Faced Woman*, didn't make money, MGM let her go—the most beautiful woman in the world, the most talented actress. No queen was ever as queenly as she.

I remember that she was my ideal even when I was young. She had such physical grace and style, and to think that people today regard her as strange! It would have been terrible for her to go to Bergdorf's, for they would have all either clustered about her or ignored her completely, and she didn't want or need that. If she dressed in baggy sweaters, why not? She might as well have been comfortable. She certainly did credit to all those Adrian gowns back in *Mata Hari* and *The Painted Veil*. Anyway, Garbo had no need for clothes, because all she did was go on long walks.

Valentina, the designer, lived on the floor above, and the two of them shared her husband, George Schley, for many years. One summer George would go with Greta to Cap Ferrat, and the next to Venice with Valentina. It might have seemed a strange relationship, but George handled all of

Joan Fontaine and Olivia de Havilland, ca. 1975, by Ellen Graham

Greta's business affairs, too, and the three of them got along very well. Lots of odd arrangements work out.

Olivia de Havilland

I met Great Garbo once, and I saw her again one night at Maxim's. That was very exciting, I can tell you. She looked quite wonderful, in a sort of sea-foam green, and she was with George Schley. Oh, she looked lovely, and she had this lovely atmosphere about her.

The first time I saw her she was wearing black, and it was at Lady Mendl's during the war. She was talking to Ludwig Bemelmans, and I wanted to meet her, but I was feeling shy about that. Then he insisted that I come forward, once he saw me there, and he introduced me. I said, "How do you do?" and that's about all, because I left, and I didn't want to interrupt their conversation. I knew it would be very difficult for me to strike up a rapport with her.

Ah, she was a wonderful actress, just marvelous. In fact, she was absolutely incomparable. And I think there isn't an actor who won't agree with me on that one. She was simply something above and beyond and apart from all the rest. She was the true empress. I thought of Bette Davis as the queen at that time, which was when Katharine Hepburn's career was sort of on the wane, you know, for she went through a very bad time, and then came back, as you know, stronger than ever. So during that time of the late thirties I thought of Garbo as the empress and Bette as the queen.

Geraldine Fitzgerald

When I finished *Wuthering Heights* I got a message saying that Miss Garbo would like to meet me. I was terribly honored by this, and it was arranged that a mutual friend would bring me for tea, but it never materialized. I did see her very close one time in a restaurant. She was simply amazingly beautiful. She had all kinds of things that most people don't have, among them long, black eyelashes. They were at least a quarter of an inch long, I'm sure, and real. She had on no makeup, but the whole way her face was constructed was so wonderful. She was an absolute goddess. She was a curious combination of being shy and liking to be open. She liked to try on hats without any other clothes. They used to have these tours through the Metro lot, and one time a tour came into the fitting room. Well, there on a high chair, trying on hats, completely nude, was Garbo. And there was no reason why she shouldn't. The relationship between an actor and a mirror is very close indeed. It would have made a wonderful picture.

Gregory Peck

One time I walked into Leland Hayward's office, in a bungalow on Wilshire Boulevard, where he had a partnership with a man named Nat Deverich. Leland had a rather elite group of clients: Joan Fontaine, and Ingrid Bergman, and Joe Cotten, and of course Garbo. As I stepped into his office that time I saw a familiar figure walking out through a pair of French doors toward the parking lot. I said to Leland that the girl looked like Garbo, and he said that it was.

It was my only glimpse of her until many years later, in about 1975, when we were at a beautiful garden party at the palace in Monaco. It was a moonlit evening under the palm trees, with lots of beautiful women in beautiful gowns, and champagne being served on the lovely grounds. One of Grace's ladies-in-waiting came up to me and said, "There is an old friend of yours here, and I'm sure you'd like to say hello." I said, "And who's that?" She said, "Why, it's Miss Garbo." Well, I had never really met her, as I explained, "But I'd like to." Véronique and I were taken over to her, and she looked fantastic in a beautiful gown in the Monaco moonlight. She was well up into her sixties at that point, I guess, and she still looked beautiful, with a lovely smile. The lady said to her, "Miss Garbo, I understand that you and Mr. Peck have never met." She replied, in that deep, romantic tone, "No, but we meet at last, and so far from home." Well, it was a scene right out of one of her movies.

It kind of knocked me out, because I've always thought that she was the best screen actress ever. Nobody could ever do what she could do. She was the greatest who ever lived. So, I was tickled to death to meet her, and we chatted a bit. She spoke in French with Véronique, and rather playfully she asked, "When you make love, does he say '*Je t'aime*' to you?" Véronique was so stunned by this that she could hardly respond. Finally she said, "Now what do you mean by that?" She didn't want to give a straight answer to such a strange question, and Garbo laughed.

I thought that it was the beginning of a beautiful friendship, and so I suggested that she come to our place for lunch. "Oh, I would love to," she replied, just as another lady came up with the whole Heineken beer family—Mr. Heineken, Mrs. Heineken, and all the little Heinekens. So, we got elbowed aside, and although I did follow through with a telephone invitation, she never came. She was staying in a villa with Valentina and George Schley at Cap d'Ail. But it didn't go anywhere. There was no response. That's the extent of my relationship with Greta Garbo.

I love to watch her movies, and I get downright indignant every time I read an interview with Rouben Mamoulian. He always talks about the final close-up in *Queen Christina*, when the ship is pulling away and she is out on the prow, having sacrificed herself and her throne for her lover, who is now dead, having lost a duel for her honor. She's heading off for a convent in Rome. Supposedly she asked Rouben, "What shall I think about?" He claims he said, "Don't think about anything. The camera loves you, and the picture will conclude with a long close-up of you." Well, by saying this and repeating it he meant to take all the credit for himself, but I've been around long enough to know that an empty close-up is an empty close-up. If there's nothing on your mind, it shows. You can be entranced by looking at this beautiful woman, but there has to be something going on upstairs for it to be so moving. If there is not, the whole thing falls flat, no matter how lovely her features are. What she was able to do was to have her train of thought photographed.

She had terrific concentration and innate good taste, and a very deeply romantic nature. She understood the man/woman thing very well. Her mind was working, and that plus her beauty was captured by the camera. In my mind she was the most beautiful woman ever on the screen, *and* the best screen actress. With that combination there is really no one who can touch her, no one who comes even close.

Scene Three

Appetizers

A S THE CLOCK STRIKES SIX the sun begins its flaming descent into the Pacific, while the two dozen guests slowly make their way back to the Casa Grande and through its ornate Vestibule. As they parade past Imperial Roman mosaics and neoclassical French statues into the cavernous Assembly Room, their astounded gasps echo throughout the vaulted chamber.

Along the walls hang immense seventeenth-century Flemish tapestries from the studio of Peter Paul Rubens, while across the floor antique Kerman, Tabriz, and Meshed carpets mute their footsteps in this incomparable museum. Opulently carved English choir stalls hug the stone walls, while towering German silver candelabra and flamboyant Italian alabaster sculptures festoon the massive tables that divide the eighty-three-foot-long parlor.

An appetizer buffet has been positioned against a monumental French Renaissance fireplace, and in front of it a statue of Venus by Antonio Canova is absorbing the rays of orange sunlight that pierce the vast window behind her. The waiters remain sure that Mr. Hearst will make his appearance at any moment, and they propose smoked salmon, pâté de foie gras, and king crab mousse.

While the cuisine is exceptional, the conversation of this movable feast is far more captivating to the Hollywood Royals whom the invisible mogul has cast in this extraordinary production. Not to be outdone by the universal worship of Garbo, Bette Davis launches into an evaluation of her own career, much as Katharine Hepburn did in the opening scene, and this appraisal leads her colleagues to reveal their own impressions of the formidable actress.

The opinions about this fiery legend nearly lead her into a confrontation with First Lady of the American Stage Helen Hayes, but then it is Davis herself who shifts the focus on to Vivien Leigh, which in turn creates a nostalgic review of *Gone With the Wind* and its star, Clark Gable. The course concludes with a look at one of his great comedies, *It Happened One Night*, and his last picture, *The Misfits*.

Bette Davis

Well, you simply can't have everything. You might be able to create a career, if you try very hard and are determined. But you cannot sustain it if you try to have a normal family life as well. There are different kinds of fulfillment, and I surely had more than most, I dare say. But happiness is difficult to find. I did have wonderful children, and of course four husbands. But there is no question about it: I gave up a lot for it. I didn't have any of the high school friends others did. I never got to go to the proms, because I was working toward my goal of becoming a great actress. I had started working even at that age.

A career like mine requires total concentration and commitment, so you really cannot have everything that you may think life holds for you. It is absolutely necessary to make a choice between professional life and personal life. On the other hand, giving up these things did not bother me at all. I simply do not regret. But I have often wondered if it might not have been a better thing to have done, to have stayed with the theater longer and not to have come to California when I was so young.

I didn't have a lucky break like Miss Hepburn, even though I had a contract. For the first few years I worked very hard to act in a lot of largely worthless pictures, but I fell in

Bette Davis, ca. 1934

love with the medium. Oh, I think that film is so superior to theater. But then, I'll never know if I made a mistake or not. It worked out. Yes, in its opportunities the screen is completely superior to the stage. In a film you can start out looking sixteen and end up at the end of the story looking forty-five. But in the theater you haven't time for all that makeup change.

Yes, I do love the art and craft of film, even though most theater people looked down upon Hollywood and the movie people. Basically they still do, even though there is hardly any theater to speak of these days. Back then, though, there was such an attitude by the theater people, even though Mr. Stewart and Mr. Fonda, after becoming great movie stars, went back to Broadway and between the two of them saved the American theater. And that was just to show the theater people that they could act, that Hollywood wasn't just sort of a playground. It's about hard work, and real talent, and total commitment. That makes a star.

Katharine Hepburn

If you keep afloat long enough, you're bound to be noticed. And I've been very fortunate in getting so many good parts. You have to realize that I've had more opportunity, though, because of the passage of time. But then you have to do what interests you, not because you think it will bring you success. It takes decision of purpose to choose your material. I think that everyone has to row his or her own boat, and that people admire someone who is rowing the boat, with a broken paddle and a hole in the bottom, because it's everyone's hope that you will keep going. Eventually they have to feel you're sort of reliable. I admire that in people, who keep rowing to the best of their ability, who keep on going.

Bette Davis

Of course, I've had my feelings hurt many times by the things people have written about me. There isn't one actor alive who hasn't been terribly hurt by critics or gossip columnists. But you get used to it, and you must accept it, for it is all part of the business. It all goes into a film career, so you learn not to beef about it, and you go on with your work and your life.

Katharine Hepburn

You know, over the years the critics have been both a help and a hindrance to me. I've never been a critic's favorite. One tends to forget that a review is only one man's opinion. It's shocking that one man has the power to close a play or ruin a film by writing a nasty review. So much money is at stake, and so many feelings and careers are tied up in it.

Since 1930 I have never read a review about me. At that time I was doing the play *Death Takes a Holiday* on Broadway, and I was referred to as "the skeleton girl with the rasping voice." The playwright, Philip Merivale, told me not to read reviews ever again. Reviews can be quite controversial, and provocative, which is good if it brings people to the theater. But in the case of that play, the material was good. Stuff like *A Woman Rebels* is really pretty boring, but I did it, back in 1936, and *Break of Hearts* the year before, not really knowing what I was doing. I did them because my agent arranged for me to do them, but I never liked them from the start.

Bette Davis

Did you ever see *Ex-Lady*? Those films that Warners put me in were really something else. I mean I was in fine casts sometimes, with James Cagney and Spencer Tracy, but the scripts themselves were generally awful. That is of course why I eventually went to England, for I knew that I would never get to play what I wanted, what I was meant to play, as long as they were giving me those parts in films like *Parachute Jumper* and *Special Agent* back in the early thirties.

But as for critics and columnists, you have to worry only when they stop talking about you. When they no longer write about you you're in trouble in this game. My mother always said to me, whenever some horrific thing that was untrue was published about me, "Don't forget, Bette: it's the best fruit the birds pick at first!" That was true. These writers can make great reputations for themselves by writing nasty things about people who are already famous. They like to invent ugly stories. You must remember that today's newspaper is tomorrow's toilet paper.

Lauren Bacall

Bette Davis was my idol when I was a kid, and then later on I became very familiar with Katie. I recall seeing Katharine Hepburn on the stage in *The Philadelphia Story* in 1939. I was sitting up in the second balcony in a fifty-five-cent seat, and she was thrilling. But Davis is the one I identified with as far as acting was concerned, back when I was in high school. Once I went to visit Bette, too, when she was staying at the Gotham Hotel on Fifth Avenue. It was an hysterical meeting, and I don't think she's recovered yet, after fifty years.

She is still quite a character, very determined and strong, and she refuses to concede an inch. I suppose that that is what has kept her alive. She's had a lot of rotten things happen to her, especially in the last few years, and she's risen above it all. In my view she's one of the all-time great movie stars and actresses. I thought she was a great beauty, too. I just loved her looks. Finally, the truth is that her career is all she had. It's what keeps her going, after four failed marriages and her daughter writing that book about her. You see what actors have to put up with.

Olivia de Havilland

Bette Davis was a very great star and a brilliant professional, and I learned from her about conversations on the set of *It's Love I'm After*, the first picture I did with her, back in 1937. For the most part, Bette avoided conversations. I was used to chatting with everyone, with the makeup man in the morning, and I would be exhausted on the set. And I couldn't figure out why. Well, it was all that talking on the set. You see, she was eight years older, and more experienced than I. Of what interest would I be to her, a great star like that? None whatsoever. She would say good morning to me, but in any case I had nothing to say to her, and she was saving her energy in an intelligent way.

One thing she did do, though, was that she always liked to see what other people were doing, and she wanted to see how I was developing my character in the movie. So, one day she came onto the set very early on in the shooting, and she said, "What does she think she's doing?" And Archie Mayo, who was directing *It's Love I'm After*, said, "Oh, no, she's a very good comedienne. Don't worry about her. It's going to be all right." Well, that fascinated me, and Archie Mayo handled it very well by defending me, for I was not doing what she thought I would do in that film. Nor was it what she would have done in that scene. Well, anyway, we had a very formal relationship, which was partly my doing, too, because I was in awe of her, and I didn't chat with Leslie Howard, either, I can tell you, for he was even more prestigious than Bette back then.

In any case, I remained in awe of Bette, and every time she did a film I went and studied it. Later on we made *In This Our Life* together, and she had just had a kind of tense and tumultuous experience with Miriam Hopkins, doing *The Old Maid*. So, Bette expected a competitive relationship with me, too, like she had had with Miriam. Well, that's not my bag at all. I can't be engaged in two arenas at once, and I don't think that's the idea anyway. So, Bette came onto the set, and it was my first scene, late in the day, and I was climbing the stairs with a suitcase, kind of overwrought. John Huston was there, too. I was supposed to get up the stairs, set down the suitcase, and ring the doorbell. I was wearing little white gloves and white shoes, and a little navy suit. Well, Bette appeared, and sat down right under the camera with a look of such challenge on her face. And I could feel her think to herself, with a sneer of imperious contempt, "Well, there's another Miriam, and I'll have to show her!" I saw this, and I thought to myself, "I know what you've been through, but I am not Miriam Hopkins, and I will never be Miriam Hopkins, and I do not choose to have with you a relationship that in any way resembles that which you have just had with Miriam Hopkins."

I knew that she had just thrown down the gauntlet, so I turned slowly and looked at her in a sort of doelike way, and I could see that she was sort of puzzled, because she wasn't getting any fight from my attitude at all. I may even have smiled and nodded to her, but I do remember that I wanted to convey to her that there would be no competition between the two of us—we would both be playing our parts, and that would be enough. Well, it worked. The next day she had a very difficult scene, a continuation of the one I had started with the doorbell. She was lying there in bed, going through a great crisis, having had an automobile accident, and on top of that she has wrongly accused someone of something, so that's on her mind.

I stood by the bed, watching this great actress whose work I so admire, wanting to know how she goes about her art. I was so close to her that she could feel my respect, admiration, expectation, and hope that she would be wonderful in the part. I could sense that she was feeling something like this, and she was just marvelous. I thought to myself, "By golly, she's as good up close as she is on the screen." They say that some artists seem to be doing nothing, and yet the camera registers something extraordinary. I wanted to know if that was in any way involved with her work, and it wasn't, for she was just astounding in person, too. We became friends on that production, and we still are.

Douglas Fairbanks, Jr.

Bette Davis did *Parachute Jumper* with me in 1933. If you haven't seen it, you're lucky. Actually, Bette was very nice, and she had come from New York not long before that, so she was like the new girl on the block. It was just a routine picture in which I was the star and she my leading lady. We got along very well, but I don't even recall the plot. That was the only movie I ever made with her, but I did produce a picture that she appeared in with her husband Gary Merrill. It was called *Another Man's Poison* and we did it in London. It was a mystery story.

James Cagney

In 1934 I played *Jimmy the Gent* with Bette Davis under Michael Curtiz, and it was my first film with comedic overtones. Very few people know this, but roles of that type were my favorites, and I always wished that they would give me more like them, because with comedy it was possible to hoke it up. That was also the picture where I showed up on the set with my hair all cut off in protest against the moviemaking conditions of the time. I had also gotten the makeup man to paint white scars all over the back of my head. I had a hell of a good time pulling that prank. When the camera picked up the scars, Curtiz almost had a Hungarian fit.

I know that Bette Davis thought I was a really tough guy, a rough character who beat up women, so she refused to be photographed with me for publicity stills. She seemed rather difficult to work with, from my point of view, but she did a good job in her part. I've said before that I thought she was a great actress, up there with Spencer Tracy, even though we didn't get along. I later made *The Bride Came C.O.D.* with her, too, in 1941.

Geraldine Fitzgerald

Bette and I became friends in 1938 while making *Dark Victory*. She was always very kind to actors. She had been a great help to Humphrey Bogart, and she was a great help to me as well. She had a reputation for being selfish and mean to others, but that was a total untruth about her. I found her to

James Cagney, ca. 1936

be humane and considerate, and I never saw her being impossible, as many people claim she was. She was always terribly generous to me.

Perhaps people got the impression that she was being testy because of her habit of repeating what you said after you said it. I think that that was simply because she wanted to be sure she had gotten what you had said to her. I know that younger actors who sometimes say silly things might think that she was making fun of them, by repeating what they had said as if to show them how foolish they were. I remember that once she was asked by Edmund Goulding, the director of *Dark Victory*, to stand "over there." She retorted with "Over there?" And then she went over there and stood like she was asked to do. Eddie was famous for making films that had a lot of heart, so he really was the perfect director for that one. It had quite a cast, too, with Ronald Reagan, and Humphrey Bogart, and George Brent. Brent was an Irish lad who came to America because he had been in some trouble connected with the political problems in Ireland. I found George Brent very hard to get to know, very removed and withdrawn.

Bette Davis

I think that George Brent was one of the most attractive men that this town had, but I certainly do not think that he was a great actor. Nor did he. He didn't care to be or to be thought of as a great actor. He was never interested in all that. He was just a wonderful, attractive Irishman. It's too bad that he did not want to have an important career, for I do think that he could have had one if he had gone after it. He simply took the money and ran, which is too bad, but then that was all he was interested in about making films. He was good when he wanted to be. He was marvelous in *Dark Victory*, for he loved the part, as my doctor, whom I married. Otherwise, he just kind of dogged it. But he liked the story of *Dark Victory*.

He was good in *Jezebel*, too, but he was not a very ambitious man, not at all. He would rather own apartment houses and make money by not working. He was a very big business-man, and the two professions really do not go together. To be a great success in the movie business one must really care about the art of it, more than the money. As George Brent once said about the era, "The only thing an actor has to worry about is his barber doing the back of his head well." That is true enough, too, for in all those love scenes in the movies the kiss was shot over the shoulder of the man and into the face of the woman. I always have felt that that was a wonderful remark.

Geraldine Fitzgerald

I understand that Bette had a little romance with George, for she was just getting over her divorce at the time we were making *Dark Victory*. I know that she was deeply upset by the divorce, so perhaps she needed someone. She was, after all, supporting her whole family, including her mother and her sister. She continued to do so until they were all dead, and I get so indignant when people ask why she does such trash, but it is because she still has children and relations to support. She looks after a lot of people.

Carroll Baker

I also worked with Bette Davis, on a Disney film called *Watcher in the Woods*, which we shot in London. I've got to say that it was a great pleasure. I went onto the set with such reverence for her, thinking that I would be polite but keep my distance, and not impose on her in any way. This was in 1979, before her stroke. Well, she was the one who was so friendly, and I had promised myself that I would not ask her all the questions about her films and the time she spent at Warners, but she volunteered it. She also held a press conference, since so many members of the British press wanted to see her and talk to her. She actually insisted that I be a part of the press conference. She was absolutely marvelous. I have seen her in her dealings with people, and as long as you are a part of the business, since she loves the business so much, she is open. She would actually sit on the set even when she wasn't required, just to cheer everyone else on.

Robert Stack

Bette was very nice when we made *John Paul Jones*, in which she appeared as Catherine the Great. The picture was okay, I suppose, and the color of it was pretty good, but there she was, handing out cigars to everyone, since my son was born during the making of it, and I was playing the title role. She was sweet to do that.

Rossano Brazzi

I was always sorry that I never worked with Bette Davis, but I know her. There was another lady whom I knew, who one day saw *Summertime*, which I made with Katharine Hepburn. Then she went to see it nine more times. That was Loretta Young. She then invited me to her house in Hollywood, a beautiful mansion done in the old style. When I got there Bette Davis was waiting for me with Loretta Young. That was when I came to know both of those ladies.

Actually, I used to see Bette Davis at the homes of people who were not connected with the movie business; one was a lawyer, and another a doctor, and another a businessman. Then I heard that Bette Davis didn't see too many people socially. She remained somewhat aloof from the whole Hollywood crowd, and all of them thought that she was rather strange. I would say that probably she is a bitter woman, but still a great actress. I think that she is the toughest of them all.

Joan Fontaine

Bette and I were on a Tail Waggers' Committee together during the war. Antivivisection, as I recall. She and Miriam

Hopkins both fought for their rights in those days. It didn't help Miriam, but Bette went to court several times and won her struggle. She may be a lady who doesn't mind a fight. She may even enjoy one. I don't. Anything ugly is anathema to me. Perhaps I'm a coward, but I prefer just to walk away. It's turning the other cheek, as they say, avoiding the fight.

In the case of Bette's daughter's book, *My Mother's Keeper*, the curator of the Boston University Library, where both Bette's and my own papers are on file, told me that Bette's daughter, B.D., had come to her with a check for $150,000 from the publisher, and said that if Bette would give B.D. the same amount then B.D. would tear up the publisher's check. Bette just shut the door, because that's just the beginning of blackmail. Grotesque! Should anyone ever try to defame me after I'm gone, the curator has been asked to deny any false statements, based on the letters and documents I have left there. I'm a saver, and everything from when I was eight is on file there.

Geraldine Fitzgerald

Bette had an awful time with her daughter's book, and a stroke, and cancer. She's got guts, and I think she's great, just great. You know, one of the children whom she adopted, the girl, turned out to be retarded, and Bette could very well have sent her back, but she didn't. The girl was only about six months old, and Bette could have done it without any loss of honor, and then gotten another child, but it was because her own sense of honor was so strict. She had high standards in everything she ever did. About twenty years ago she decided to put the girl into a home, to make sure that she was taken care of after she herself was gone. She left enough money there to support the girl, who grew up, for the rest of her life. It's a very special private place, not a state home. You have to apply the word "great" to Bette, for she is. Every time I see one of her old pictures she seems to have improved, which I know is of course impossible, but nonetheless, that is how it seems.

Olivia de Havilland

In 1964, when Joan Crawford, who did have a very competitive relationship with Bette, didn't go through with *Hush . . . Hush, Sweet Charlotte*, and ended up in an oxygen tent, they called me in Switzerland and asked me if I would do the part. I knew it was a very important production, along the lines of *What Ever Happened to Baby Jane?*, but I told them I'd have to read the script. Well, Bette called and said, "I just hope you say yes." Then Robert Aldrich came with the script, which I read, and I said to him that I just couldn't do it, because this character was all dark, and on top of that she was rude. He said that he wished I would read it again, and I said, "Mr. Aldrich, when I make up my mind I never change it."

Well, he pleaded with me to read it again, saying that he was surprised I hadn't seen the dichotomy of character. I told him that I didn't see any ambivalence in the way it was written. During the night I got another idea, because I read it again, and it kind of haunted me, even though I still thought that she was an awful psychopath, and rude to boot! And if she wasn't the villainess, which she seemed to be from the very first scene, then you wanted her to be, because she was so rude to everyone.

I spoke to Aldrich again the next day, and told him that there was one way to play her, to give her the quality he saw, but which I didn't, and I explained it to him. "Suppose you give her perfect manners. You wouldn't have to change a single scene. All you would have to do is to take out her rudeness," I proposed. "One word, one phrase, one line here and there. That's all. If you do that you keep the suspense going for the audience, for the way it's written they guess what's going on from the first scene." He thought about that, and I continued, "Where's the suspense the way you have it now? They *know* she's guilty if she's rude. And look how this

Olivia de Havilland, *The Great Garrick*, 1937

will work for Bette, too." He said to me, "I like your idea, and I'm going back right away, and I'll phone you." Of course he had to talk to Bette first, but she saw that it made sense, for this way we could keep the suspense up right until the very last scene. I was pretty sure that Crawford understood that something was going wrong, and didn't know why, and that was what made her sick. She knew she had to get out of that project, and she was right to get out of it the way it was planned. The part, as it was written, would have made a catastrophe of the film. They were trying to do the reverse of *Baby Jane*, and it was wonderful showmanship in putting the two of them together again, but they tackled the role all wrong. I guess they wanted to give it some variety from the other part, in which she was always so gentle and polite.

Well, the only way to do that was to keep her polite, and then pull the surprise, which was that she was really the wicked one who had killed the boyfriend. That's the way we did it, and again I learned from Bette. A young Englishman had done a rewrite on the script, and that's the one they had sent to me. We worked it all out so that we would have rehearsals on the weekend, and that was wonderful. Before we started shooting I said that I wanted to see the footage of Crawford in the part, and I did, and it was all dark. And she was so rude right away, to Agnes Moorehead, who played the slattern. Well, the audience is not going to care for anyone who is rude to her. Anyway, I could see Crawford struggling, because she could see that it was all going wrong. She could feel it, but she didn't know why, even though it was just a mechanical thing, just a question of manners. A simple thing like that. So, I knew that I was on the right track.

The weekend before we were to start shooting we all got together at Bette's, with the young writer, and Bette went over speech after speech that he had written for her. "We don't need this, and we don't need that," she would say, just tossing whole sections of her part away. She would slash her own part to bits, saving only the lines that counted, maybe two sentences out of a whole paragraph of dialogue. She knew she didn't need that much to say, since she could convey so much without speaking. She was just wonderful. Her spirit is still extraordinary, even after all of her illness and operations. And at the time her daughter's book came out she was in the hospital! Well, that hurt her very deeply, because she had a wonderful relationship with her daughter. I've seen them together, back when she got engaged, and Bette was wonderful to her. I wouldn't read that book she wrote.

Not long ago Bette was in Paris, and she said she wanted to have dinner. I didn't have any domestic help at home, but I said, "Well, yes, of course" when she asked me. All the florists were closed, since it was in August, and she said that she wanted to bring her secretary, too, for her to see my house, which she said she loved. Oh, I was tripping all over myself to set the table and polish the silver, with only one student helping. Well, I did the whole thing, cooking a dish that could be reheated and set on the table, family-style, but nonetheless with the silver butter dishes and that kind of thing. I knew that she liked to drink ahead of time, so I had white wine and soda. She doesn't like champagne.

Well, she was fifteen minutes early, and I was stark naked upstairs. I had just gotten out of the tub, and thought I had fifteen minutes to put on my dress. My assistant, Paul, was polishing the last tray in the dining room when he called up to me, "My God, she's here!" I shouted down to let her in and to pour the wine spritzer, and then I made it down in four minutes. She was sitting, but wouldn't take anything to drink until I got there. I was exhausted, since I finally found some flowers at five o'clock that afternoon, but it was wonderful to be with her. She was so gallant and full of spirit, and she talked about the book. "Have you read it?" she asked, even though she was so upset by it. I said, "No, and I wouldn't think of reading it!" So she said, "Well, I think you should!"

She's just fabulous, a truly remarkable woman. A fellow could feel very protective of her, but she won't accept protectiveness from me for a minute. I can remember my feeling about her when I was sixteen and I saw her for the first time on the screen. She was such a dynamic creature, not one of those conventional heroines at all, and I just thought to myself "Who is *that*? That's somebody extraordinary, and I'm going to watch her work!" Well, two years later I was on the Warners lot working with her! Now what do you make of that?

Lauren Bacall

Bette Davis came to see me do *Applause* on Broadway, which was based on *All About Eve*, one of her greatest films. I didn't know she was there, and I probably would have fainted if I had known she was in the audience. Afterward she came backstage, and she was very polite, though not filled with wild enthusiasm. She said to me, "I knew that if anyone could do this you could." Life's turns are often quite amusing, aren't they? I've always felt that *Applause* was a much better piece than *Woman of the Year*. The whole thing worked much better, although *Woman of the Year* was also very successful. Katie came to see me do her part, too. But that was weird, wasn't it? First playing Bette's role in *Applause*, and then doing Katie's role in *Woman of the Year*, both of them musicals based on straight plays. My life has been very peculiar, and I don't claim to understand it. I don't even pretend to.

James Stewart

Bette is much more than gifted. We had a great time making *Right of Way*, about an elderly couple who just wanted to die. She was not in very good shape at the time, but she's determined to keep at it. She's that type of person, and she just won't let it get her down, for this is her work, which I think is very admirable. I thought she was wonderful in *The Whales of August*, too, which she made not long ago with Ann Sothern and Lillian Gish.

Lillian Gish

We got along all right on that one, I'd say. I did everything I could do to please her, of course. I don't recall ever having had an actor or an actress with whom I couldn't get along. I've never thought about my being first or second in the billing, and I never brought up the fact that my name should be used, above *or* below the title. If it wasn't used it was better for me, I thought, because of my family. I just never had any big head about "me," and I always felt that I was so lucky. Everyone was so good to me throughout my career, and I can say in all honesty that I don't recall having had a quarrel with anyone ever.

Helen Hayes

I never got to know Bette until a few years ago, when we did a "Miss Marple" movie, and it wasn't funny. She was still the temperamental, difficult woman, even after all the years and all the success. Even in her heyday that kind of behavior was unwelcome, so she made many enemies and created an awful impression, when she never needed to do so. Though she may have been wonderful in her seventies, it was not nearly so evident as it was when she was in her twenties and thirties. She was so imperious when we made *Murder by Mirrors* in 1984, and very tough to get along with. Johnny Mills was in that picture, too, and when we came to the end of it I said to him, during a quiet moment when we were sitting on a sofa together, "Johnny, have you enjoyed it at all?" In very distinct and deliberate tones he replied, "I have never been so frightened in my entire life."

I think we were all frightened by Bette. You never knew when she was going to insult you. The poor dear, she just can't stop it. It sounds funny, but it's not; it's just awful. We were all scared of her, but I kept telling myself, "I'm going to win this one. I cannot have this kind of stress. I must have some peace of mind if I'm going to make this picture and

P.1457-1

Helen Hayes, ca. 1931

survive." After all, I was eighty-four. So, I set out to be a bit
friendly, because after all I adored her and her work. I was
simply not of a mind to have a feud with her. I also respected
her for knowing her business, which I didn't. So, I was in the
perfect frame of mind to become a good friend to someone
whom I admired. I thought that I was doing all right as we
went along, and then finally one day she said to me, "You are
a beautiful person." Well, I thought that this was like a
diploma *magna cum laude* from Oxford, just the highest thing
you could get. So, we finished the picture friends, and I
thought that everything was just lovely.

Then one of those damned columnists called me, just
before the picture came out, and asked me, "What on earth
was wrong with Bette Davis when you two were doing that
picture? She looked ghastly!" I was down in Mexico at the
time I got the call, and was asked if I had seen the film, and I
said that I had not. "Well, Bette was a mess, just terrible, and
it was agonizing to watch her," this columnist said to me. I
replied that I felt that Bette had not really wanted to do the
picture, for I knew that they had had a hard time getting her
deal worked out to her satisfaction.

The film was made in England, and she wouldn't even
come to the set until she was sure the clothes fit her, so they
had to send the designer to Hollywood to make her clothes for
her there. They ended up having to send the fitters back and
forth between England and California three times before they
could get her costumed. At last she agreed that they suited
her, so she went to England, and there she tore them all apart,
claiming that they didn't fit her. She refused to step onto the
set until everything was absolutely right. She had to have her
hairdresser brought over from California, and then her makeup man had retired and gone to live in the south of Spain, so
he had to be flown up from there. All of these problems had to
be dealt with before she would consider going onto the set.
She definitely did not look well, for she had had that stroke as
well as breast cancer. She really wasn't completely straightened out, but the producers kept pushing her before she was

ready to do anything in front of a camera. They liked the idea of our two names together, so they kept after her. It didn't matter to them that she wasn't well, and in fact not really right for the part.

So, this columnist was on the phone asking me about Bette, and I said, "Well, maybe they pushed her too hard. Maybe she came back too soon, I don't know." Do you know that that woman put it into her column that Helen Hayes said that Bette Davis came back too soon? Well, Bette called me in Mexico and said, "You have been very unkind to me. You have said unkind things about me." I responded by asking her what I had said, since I had not seen the column or even heard about it. Well, I couldn't stand there and tell her the circumstances, that I had been misquoted, that it was out of context, that the columnist had seen the film and said that Bette looked dreadful, for that would have heaped insult on top of injury. So, I just let it go, and there went that friendship.

Bette thought that I had done her in—but then, she thought that everyone had done her in. She thought that everyone was out to do her in. She was in the same state of mind with Lillian Gish too, when they made *The Whales of August*. She was horribly insulting to Lillian, who is as sweet a lady as I have ever met, and unable to defend herself verbally. Bette was just frightful to Lillian in the making of that picture. She really is something. Being a major movie star is a tough life, and she more than any other actress has just let the drive and ambition dominate her. She is not alone in this character trait, but she is probably the most remarkable example of it. The life and job are hard, and eventually they no longer have any outside life beyond the movies.

My good friend Norma Shearer went completely overboard after her career stopped. She just couldn't deal with life. We were quite close, and she was very dear to me. In fact, my husband, Charles MacArthur, and I went on long trips abroad with Norma and her husband, Irving Thalberg. She couldn't conduct her life without the prop of the screen. I don't know exactly what happened, if she lost her mind or just retreated into seclusion. Back in the early thirties she was always citing me as her best friend, but when she retired I was completely cut off. I tried, but I couldn't get near her. She disappeared, and I don't know if she couldn't navigate or cope any longer or what was going on.

Bette and Norma both led lives that were wrapped up in celluloid, and it ate them up. By contrast, I was out there for only about five years, so I got in and got out before it devoured me. I know one thing, though, that if I had been an actress whose whole life had been centered on film I might have joined the cocaine train. I think a lot of them keep going with the help of drugs. The work is so hard, and the pressure so great. You just cannot keep those hours and still have something special to give the camera. How I hated that life out there, that way of working! I hated everything about it, and I couldn't wait to come back to New York and the Broadway stage.

Bette Davis

I always said that if any movie actor or actress went back to the theater it was because he or she couldn't get a suitable part in a film. That is why I went back to Broadway; there was absolutely nothing around that was any good that I could do. I mean, to leave a nice home where the weather is always so lovely? Actually, I was the first actress offered *A Streetcar Named Desire*, but I had just had a child, and I had a nice home, and I loved making films, so I turned it down, and Jessica Tandy did it. I didn't want to disrupt my very pleasant and secure life at that point, but I've often wondered if in fact I should have accepted the offer. It was a great play, and if I had done the play I might have been asked to do the movie as well, which Vivien Leigh did with Mr. Brando.

Geraldine Fitzgerald

Vivien Leigh and Laurence Olivier were madly in love at the time we were making *Wuthering Heights*. I didn't know her then, although she did come onto the set and watch us shoot. It was years later, after Larry and Vivien got divorced, and she was having an affair with John Merivale, the son of the playwright Philip Merivale, that I saw a lot of her. He took very good care of her, since she was not well, but she used to come for tea with me. I got to know her very well then, and she told me that she thought she had no business on the stage with Olivier. She said that she felt deeply embarrassed when she was, and was sure that the audience was thinking to themselves that they wished she would get off. She thought that they were there to see only Larry. I told her that she had the power to light up the stage when she came on. I recall saying, "Vivien, you have the rare gift of being able to throw your face from the stage right to the very last row of the theater, and that is a great talent."

Well, she couldn't believe that, and claimed that they wanted simply for her to get off and for Larry to get on. I said that they might indeed want Larry to come on, but that they never wanted for her to get off. She was simply radiant. I think that she had been through an awful lot for her to think such a thing about herself. Isn't it amazing that the most beautiful ones think they're ugly, and the most talented ones think they have nothing to offer? She was only a year older than I, and truly beautiful. Nice features in themselves simply do not constitute beauty. She had that inner light, but she thought she was not beautiful, and felt that her worst flaw was what she referred to as her weak chin. Of course it was perfect, like the rest of her.

Olivia de Havilland

Vivien and I were both very upset when George Cukor was replaced by Victor Fleming as the director of *Gone With the Wind*, for we didn't know Victor at the time. But I suppose that Clark had the most to lose on that picture, and Vivien had nothing to lose. She was not known, and she had no American career at all, and her British career was just budding. For her, if *Gone With the Wind* had failed, it wouldn't have mattered at all. If I had not done well in it, it would have mattered a little, but not a lot since I wasn't making it for Warner Brothers.

But if Gable failed, it would have destroyed his career, for he was at the very top, the King, and he had a huge investment in that film. We knew that all the United States and half the rest of the world had read the book and had a very clear idea about Rhett Butler, so he was very nervous. Clark was really terrified of failing that image. He knew that he had to have absolute confidence in his director, or he risked not fulfilling this immense expectation about Rhett. Now George had an erroneous reputation for being a woman's director. Jimmy Stewart won his first Oscar for *The Philadelphia Story*, which George had directed, and Ronald Colman won his only Oscar under George's direction, too, in *A Double Life*. So, this reputation was quite unfair, but he did have it, and people believed it. So I think that Clark, in his immense anxiety, felt that perhaps he ought to be directed by someone he knew, and in whom he had perfect confidence. That's why George was replaced by Victor, although it was more than just having Cukor taken off. It was partly having Fleming take over, since he was so good with action scenes, which was not George's specialty, so the company in a sense gained by the change.

Actually, I talked to Howard Hughes about this, when Howard was about to leave for Key West, in February of 1939. He took me out to dinner one night not far from MGM, and I said, "I'm terribly worried about something, for I understand that George is going to be taken off the film, and he had so much to do with Vivien's and my being chosen for the parts. He helped us to develop our characters, and we both feel so secure with him. Now he's going to be gone, and we both have these terrible responsibilities, and we don't know Victor Fleming." Well, Howard was so nice, I remember. He said to me, "Don't worry. I know Victor Fleming, and he has the same talent as George Cukor, whom I also know." He came up with a wonderful analogy about them, saying that Victor was strained through a coarser screen, and this gave me confidence in Victor. I soon saw that he was right, for Victor was much simpler in his direction, but just as true, and that was the point. Actually, I see *Gone With the Wind* from time to time still, and it never ceases to engage my full attention.

Helen Hayes

Clark Gable was just a darling if ever there was one. He was fun to be with, and fun to work with, and we laughed our way through *The White Sister*, which was no laughing matter. Actually we were laughing at the film itself, for it had a ridiculous quality about it. My very dear friend Lillian Gish, godmother of my son as well as of my first grandson, had played *The White Sister* in the silent film version. It was the most moving and impressive picture when she made it, I have to say.

Well, when I was at Metro I was assigned to make the sound version of it with Clark, under Victor Fleming's direction. But something happened in the transformation, for when you put the words into people's mouths the whole thing began to seem rather ridiculous. Now this was back in 1933, even though the story had been perfectly lovely only ten years earlier in the one Lillian made. It just didn't work on any level, so we were moved to laughter throughout the making of it, which was unfortunate. Even though it was awful, *The White Sister* left me with the impression of Clark as a merry, funny fellow.

Later that year we were together again in a David Selznick picture called *Night Flight*, based on a novel by Antoine de Saint-Exupéry. That one had a great cast, too, with both John and Lionel Barrymore as well as Robert Montgomery and Myrna Loy. I played Clark's wife in it, and Clark was determined that he and I would have a private little episode, if you follow me. He kept telling me about a secret place he had up in the Hollywood Hills where he wanted me to go with him to have a merry old time. Apparently he had an Oriental up there

Clark Gable and Jean Harlow, *Wife vs. Secretary*, 1936

to wait on us during the weekend that he was planning. I declined, however, since I was quite happily married to Charlie MacArthur.

I was so grateful to have a good marriage, and I certainly didn't want to play around with Clark, though he was very attractive, and I did enjoy his friendship. Later on, when I opened in *Victoria Regina* in California, he came and brought his wife, Carole Lombard. They came backstage to see me after the show on opening night, and I was so pleased to see him again. He teased me a bit, saying, "Helen, do you remember that when we made *White Sister* you were too shy?" That was the way he put it, which I found very endearing. I really don't think that I was too shy, but then maybe I was.

Maureen O'Sullivan

In 1932 I made *Strange Interlude* with both Clark Gable and Norma Shearer, the King and the Queen. Clark was awfully nice, and I liked him a lot. I came in on that film at the end, when my character first appeared, and I was completely green. I made no effort to move in the right direction, because I didn't know about trade papers, and I really didn't know what success meant. Even after *Tarzan* came out I didn't know that it was a success until they told me. But then I was just a kid from Ireland.

Anyway, by the time I came in Clark was in his "old" makeup, and Norma Shearer was made up like a beautiful old lady, and I just took them as they were, assuming that Clark was an old man, and that Norma was an old woman. I was very respectful of their ages, saying, "How do you do?" very politely, just as you would behave toward old people. Well, I was sitting there, waiting to say my lines, and Clark came over to sit down right beside me. I was thinking to myself that this old fellow was so sweet and kind to me. Every morning when I came in he would say, "How are you, baby?" and give me a kiss. Norma had a cast in one eye, so you never knew whether she was looking at you or not. I found that terribly interesting, to think that she might be looking at me when it seemed that she was looking the other way.

Clark didn't spend much time with her, but he did with me. One day he said to me, "I've got a good idea. Do you like to ride horseback?" I said that I did, that I rode every Sunday through the park. "Well, then, let's go out on Sunday! I'll take you out!" he beamed. "We'll have lunch together." Well, I thought to myself, "This old guy!" I imagined galloping over the hills, and him trotting ten miles behind me, and wondered what fun that would be. So I said to him, "Oh, that's really sweet, but I can't. I'm going with Leslie Howard." Well, I missed out on that date with Clark, but he asked me later to go somewhere else, and I was still thinking that he was much too old to be interesting to me, so I turned him down again. God, when I think about it! To think that I missed out on dates with Clark Gable! He never asked me again, and who can blame him, really?

After the shooting was over we had to do a lot of voice recording, since much of *Strange Interlude* is in the form of thoughts, voices without actual talking on the screen. They didn't need to photograph us for the sound of our thoughts, so we didn't have to wear any makeup and I saw this terrific young man, who was Clark Gable, and I realized what a fool I had been. Maybe he didn't like Norma's makeup, and thus talked to me so much during filming, I don't know. She had gray hair and looked ancient, so maybe that was why he turned to something sprier and younger. Once when he was talking to me I realized that Norma was watching, with her good eye or her bad, and then the assistant director came over and said, "Mr. Gable, Miss Shearer would appreciate it if you wouldn't spend so much time talking to Miss O'Sullivan." Now it could be that she thought he wasn't paying enough attention to his lines, for after all, he wasn't. Clark looked up at him and said, "Well, is that so? You can tell her what she can do! No, I'll tell her what she can do!" He jumped up and marched over to Norma and told her, and that was the end of that.

But afterward Norma and I became great friends. I was devoted to her. She was, of course, treated like the queen bee, married to Irving Thalberg, who was then head of production. I'll tell you how dear she was. She came to lunch one day when John Farrow, my previous husband, and I were living up in the top of Bel-Air, where we had built a house. She had gone to wash her hands before Sunday luncheon and I found her in the bathroom drying her hands on the shower curtain. "Norma," I said, "what on earth are you doing? There are towels right there." "I know," she replied, "but they looked so nice that I didn't want to touch them." I found that very dear, for I know I have done the same thing, when the hand towels for guests looked too nice to touch. We were very close, and she was always treated like Marie Antoinette, whom she played.

Ava Gardner

The first time I worked with Clark Gable was in 1947 on *The Hucksters*, with Adolphe Menjou and Deborah Kerr. It was her first American film, and they had a slogan to the effect of "Kerr is here and Gable's got her!" It was something like that.* In any event, I had been in love with Clark Gable ever since I was a little girl in North Carolina. I still adore him. Actually, I ended up doing three films with him, and we became very good friends, but there was never any flirtation. I would walk onto the set to do a scene, and I'd find myself opposite Clark Gable, and I would draw an absolute blank. It was so difficult to work with Clark because I was in love with him, but he was so sweet, especially when we made *Lone Star* with Lionel Barrymore in 1952.

Barrymore taught me a wonderful lesson once, when I had

---

* Ava apparently confused and combined several different MGM publicity campaigns that have become movie legends: "Gable's back and Garson's got him!" which was designed for *Adventure*, the 1946 film that heralded Gable's return to moviemaking after the war; "Finally he met a lady, but he was no gentleman," initially scheduled to promote *The Hucksters*; and "Kerr—Rhymes with Star!" which was the one finally used.

only one line in this one scene, and he was an old man in a wheelchair with arthritis. It was being shot on a back lot, and as usual there were a lot of pretty girls standing around. The script had one line, so they gave it to me. Now at five o'clock Clark and Lionel would quit, and they were the only ones who did. The rest of us just kept doing our scenes alone. Do you know that on this occasion that sweet old man stayed after five just to be there so that I would have someone to say my line to?

I learned a very important lesson in manners that day. Some actors won't do that. They just don't give a damn. But the really big stars are professionals. You can say that they might not have been the greatest actors or the greatest personalities, but by God, they were more than that. They were stars, man! I'm sorry I never had an affair with Clark, but I worshiped him as a fan, and I adored him as a person. But Clark's been gone a long time now, as have many of the other fine actors I worked with back then.

Loretta Young

Clark Gable was certainly very appealing, and one could very easily fall in love with him. He also was a wonderful man in that he was so at ease with himself, and with everybody else. As rough and tough as he played so many of those parts, you will notice that in all of those love scenes, particularly in *Gone With the Wind*, he is so gentle with women. He treats them with such tenderness, such sweetness. That to me is an unbeatable combination on the screen.

Yes, I've heard all those fifty-year-old rumors about Clark and me and our romance during the making of *The Call of the Wild* in 1935. They were rumors then, they're rumors now, and they'll always be rumors. Gossip sometimes rolls down a hill and takes on such proportions, such a life of its own, that you can't get it back up the hill. So, you can just ignore it. That was all so far in the past, too. But gossip for gossip's sake is nothing but evil, as far as I am concerned. It helps no one,

Loretta Young, ca. 1952

and it might hurt someone. I did two pictures with Clark, and the second one was *Key to the City* in 1950. As a person he was just a delight, but I didn't see him too much socially. But Clark Gable certainly was everything that he appeared to be.

Carroll Baker

I also made a film with Clark Gable called *But Not for Me*. The title was drawn from a song that went "They're writing songs of love, but not for me." He was involved with a young girl, an actress, whom I played, and his ex-wife was Lilli Palmer, who sort of smirked on the sidelines, because she felt sure that this affair would not work out. I forget exactly what happened in the picture, but I remember that he went on a binge for about three days, and finally concluded that he just couldn't be involved with the actress. All in all it was a rather innocent movie, for there were no bedroom scenes. Sometimes I believe that movies were sexier when such things were suggested, rather than depicted explicitly. *But Not for Me* came out in 1959, so it was one of Clark's last movies.

James Stewart

It was really not until after the war that I got to know Clark well, when we would play golf quite a bit. Apart from being an excellent actor, Clark was a very fine man. I have to admit that at the time I didn't realize how good he was. When I see his pictures now I am deeply impressed with his ability as an actor, for he was very serious about his work. He let the publicity department take care of the image of glamour and romance in the private life of the big star and leading man.

Actually he was sent to Columbia to do *It Happened One Night* opposite Claudette Colbert under Frank Capra as a punishment by Mayer. It was nothing serious that Clark had done, I'm sure, but rather a matter of standing up for his own rights. So, to put him in his place they farmed him out, and

look how well it worked out for him. It was an Academy
Award-winning classic that enhanced his fame. The studios
did this to a lot of their contract actors, to hire them out to
discipline them, so Mayer sent Clark down to Gower Street,
where Harry Cohn ran the Columbia studio. Back in those
days it was definitely a step down. Metro and Paramount and
Warners were the big ones, and all the others, like Columbia
and Universal and RKO, were like poor cousins. I still think
that *It Happened One Night* is one of the best pictures of all
time, so that move really backfired on Mayer, but then that
was how things happened so often back then.

Olivia de Havilland

Clark was very professional, and very strict as well, which
Vivien and I liked. He was always so well prepared, too, and
he wanted to adhere to the terms of his contract on *Gone With
the Wind*, especially about when he wanted to go home at the
end of the day. It was to be six o'clock on the dot. They would
often set up a shot at five-thirty, and I saw them try to
persuade him to stay on later, which was hard for him, for he
was a fellow who liked to be agreeable. But he stuck to his
guns and was really tough, even though he would have loved
to say yes. But he always refused, for that would have been the
thin edge of the wedge, and he knew that he had a long drive
to his home in the Valley. And then he would have a long
drive back in the morning to be on the set at nine o'clock. He
knew. He had lines to prepare, and he had Carole Lombard to
go home to.

Robert Stack

Clark Gable was like my surrogate father, and I have to say
that in person he was very much as he seemed to be on the
screen. We used to go duck shooting all the time, and one
night at the duck lodge he hauled out a bottle of twenty-one-
year-old Scotch and said, "Sit down, Bob. I want to talk to

you. I never talked to you about acting because I never knew if you would be any good. But then I saw something of yours that I thought was all right. It was *The Bullfighter and the Lady*." Well, he sat me down, and he talked about the profession and the responsibilities. "If you're ever any good it's ninety percent the other guy's fault," he said, "but the bottom line is to be a professional."

I wish that I had made a recording of that talk to play to everyone starting out in this business. I believe it's why I have a little more patience with those who seem to have been ill advised, who make poor choices in roles and projects. I had the great fortune and luxury of being advised by people who personified the right things about the business. If I had done anything wrong Gable and Tracy both would have kicked me right in the ass. No one has kicked some of these guys who have appeared overnight, and they think that they know it all as a result. They need to be kicked in the ass. Behavior is conditioned largely by association with and respect for your peers, I believe. If you associate with no one you respect, then you are going to end up nowhere. If you are IT, then you are nobody. As Gable said, "professionalism" is the one driving word, what determines everything in your career. Talent or no talent, that's up to God. Opportunity may or may not come your way, but being a pro will carry you through an entire lifetime, of mediocrity or magic, of failure or success.

Ironically, it was my darling Carole Lombard, whom I had known up at my mother's house at Lake Tahoe, where she got her divorce from Bill Powell in 1933, who treated me like a man when I was only thirteen. When she wound up getting involved with Clark it put me in an awkward position, since I was supposed to be her lover. It was a matter of to be or not to be for me. That was when the strange and confusing problems began, in 1939, when I decided to go into pictures and sort of stepped into their backyard. I was always so fond of Clark, and I liked him very much. He was what he was, like all of us. They say he was at one time a coal miner, but I don't know.

Everyone came from somewhere. Everyone had to struggle at some point.

I had a hunch when Clark went up to do *The Misfits* that he wouldn't be coming back. I knew about Marilyn, about her compulsive lateness, and sometimes not showing up at all. She often didn't know her lines, and would get so sick she would throw up. By contrast Clark was the total professional. He was always on time, and he did his own stunts, too. He told me before they started shooting that he had gone on a crash diet. "Because I'm working with Montgomery Clift," he said. Clark was much older than Monty, and yet he so respected Clift as an actor that he wanted to be able to compete one on one with him on every level.

Well, Marilyn didn't show up, which was stressful for Clark, and on top of that he was doing his own stunts, which led to his fatal heart attack. Ray Holmes used to tell me that he was afraid Clark would blow sky high, because he just wasn't used to that kind of unprofessional behavior on Marilyn's part. Sure enough, he did explode about her lateness, and then after he had the heart attack from those strenuous stunts he was in the hospital. He couldn't stand the sight of the oxygen machine in his room, so he told them to take it out. I sent him a letter in the hospital, and while it was in transit he died. I had suggested to him that we go duck hunting again, but it was too late. Had he kept that oxygen machine by his bed he might have survived, but it's too late to speculate. It was a terrible blow. When I watch the scene of Marilyn and Clark sitting in the front of that car in *The Misfits*, looking at the stars and talking of the future, I think, "What a piece of fate! The end of three of the most important careers in one film!" No, this is not a happy business.

Scene Four

Soupe Du Jour

THE CHIMES STRIKE SEVEN as Robert Stack delivers a melancholy tribute to Gable, the late King of Hollywood, and then the butler appears in his white tie and tails to invite the two dozen guests to be seated for the next course. As they pass from the sumptuous grandeur of the baroque Assembly Room they also move back into history by several centuries, for the splendid Refectory is a glorious Gothic hall that blends the whimsy of Camelot with the severity of a Romanesque abbey.

In the center of the long room a solid oak table, which looks as if it has served thousands of monks or nuns over the years, extends for forty feet like the keel of the ship of state. Twenty-four thrones fit for the Knights of the Round Table line the narrow dining board, while above it are suspended a series of gilded chandeliers. Beyond them hang silk banners from the Palio of Siena, their gay colors enlivening the sober if lordly fixtures and furnishings. Illuminated by magnificent solid silver candlesticks, the room is highlighted by the priceless sixteenth-century "Daniel" tapestries, and anchored by the silver Mace of State of the Irish Parliament, acquired by Mr. Hearst when business was booming.

The guests find their places according to cards in front of the gold-trimmed Blue Willow china, and as soon as they are all seated the staff rolls in a massive golden tureen of soup, which they identify as "Homemade Vegetable" from the gardens of exotic specimens cultivated in the acres of hothouses

115

on the grounds. Sensing that a note of levity is in order, buoyant Jack Lemmon starts off with a discussion of *Some Like It Hot* and his costar Marilyn Monroe.

This soon leads the guests to appraise director George Cukor, producer David O. Selznick, and actor David Niven. Niven's loss prompts George C. Scott to recall the gentlemanly art of Henry Fonda, and with that immortal as the subject of attention, the course ends with everyone wondering when their host will appear, and where he will sit when he does.

Jack Lemmon

I've got to say that I just loved working with Marilyn Monroe on *Some Like It Hot,* and we got along great. She was a pain in the ass to Billy Wilder, however, and especially to Tony Curtis. It was her chronic lateness that he couldn't abide. It was not her temperament, but rather a psychological problem. She could be fully dressed and made up and sitting in her dressing room right there on the soundstage, and you couldn't get her out for an hour and a half. She kept everyone waiting until she was psyched up enough to face the camera. Otherwise, she just couldn't do it. This drove Billy crazy, of course, since he had a whole company sitting there ready to work, and he was responsible for the budget. Then by the time she at last came out everyone else was exhausted from waiting, so he would have to try to get the rest of us pumped back up.

In the second half of the film I was off dancing with Joe E. Brown with a rose in my mouth, so I had no problems with Marilyn. But most of Tony's scenes were with Marilyn, and she was driving him nuts with this way of delaying and wearing him down. I did sit and talk with her now and then, and I remember distinctly feeling that she would let you get just so close before she would try and split. Being an armchair analyst I felt that she had a deep fear of being hurt again, so she was very careful about letting anyone get too close to her. I could feel how terribly unhappy she was as well. I could tell that the laughing and smiling when she relaxed was just a facade.

I know that there has been speculation that she was murdered and did not in fact commit suicide, but I have never even wanted to read all that stuff. The whole story was so bizarre that I doubt we will ever know for sure what really happened. She was certainly attractive in person, but I think that she had one of those charismatic personalities that come over much stronger on the screen than in the flesh, if you will. There was something between that lens and her that was just dynamite. During the rushes I would find myself looking at her, and I wouldn't even think to look at myself; that's how magnetic she was on film.

You know, you can try to evaluate a scene as you're doing it, as well as later in the rushes, and I can swear that at times when we were filming I would think to myself that there was nothing happening in her eyes, that she was mechanical, that the scene wasn't working. Then later in the rushes she would be like exploding dynamite. She would be absolutely terrific in the very scene we had just made when I thought that she was flat and blank. It was as if the magic went straight from her into the lens, totally invisible to the rest of us who were right there shooting it with her. Frankly, I often had the feeling that I was acting at her, but not with her. But then the scenes worked, and that's the bottom line. There are only a few of them like that, superb actors whose true brilliance comes through on the screen through the camera, but much less so, if at all, when filming.

Lauren Bacall

I made *How to Marry a Millionaire* with Marilyn back in 1953, but I have nothing to say about her except that she was sweet and sad, not bitchy at all. She was always a sad young woman reaching out for something she never could quite find. I believe that she was looking for some kind of resolution to her life.

Marilyn Monroe, ca. 1948

Marilyn Monroe, ca. 1962

Rossano Brazzi

I met Marilyn when she was starting out at Fox, and she said to me, "Mr. Brazzi, are you going to Beverly Hills?" I said that I was, and I would happily take her wherever she wanted. We became good friends at that point. She did some funny things, too. I remember that sometimes she would drive up to my house in a little white car, and my wife would notice her waiting out there, so I would have to act as if I didn't know what Marilyn wanted, parked out there in the middle of the night. One night I came home late from Fox, and my wife assumed that I had been up to something, but she was too smart to be jealous. You know, the expression "Latin Lover" was invented for me by some journalists in New York. Louella Parsons once asked Lydia, my wife, if she wasn't jealous of all these onscreen affairs I was having, and Lydia, who had a great sense of humor, said, "You know, I married Rossano when he was only nineteen years old, so if he didn't go to bed with someone else since then how would he know that I am so good?"

I realize now that I was quite handsome, but forty years ago I didn't know it. I remember going to Venice one year, and at the Danieli Hotel four thousand girls broke every window in the place, trying to get to me. I had to have bodyguards just to walk down the street. In my heyday I received twenty-five thousand letters each month.

In any case, I think that there was something unbalanced in Marilyn from the very start. I firmly believe that her death was an accident, since I was really very close to her, right up until the end. She simply couldn't sleep any longer. She had had six miscarriages by the time she died, and was simply unable to carry a child through the nine months. After all these traumas she started to take pills to get to sleep, because she desperately wanted to have a child. She had signed a contract with George Cukor, who was really a great director and a wonderful man, but with women something of a son of a bitch.

The first day of shooting *Something's Got to Give* she came one hour late, and then two hours late, and by the end of the first week she got to the set three hours late. Then she received a letter saying that she was dismissed from the film. It was Doris Day who took her place, and Doris had wanted to do *South Pacific* with me, too. Anyway, Marilyn went back home and took some pills to get to sleep, then had something to drink before falling asleep. Then she woke up after a few hours and, forgetting that she had already taken pills, took some more, which amounted to an overdose. I never thought that it was suicide or murder, but the gossip mills in Hollywood turn everything into sensational scandal.

There were two women especially in Hollywood who did this: Hedda Hopper and Louella Parsons. Louella drank a lot, by the way. One day she came to my house for dinner, and she brought along a man who wrote for *The Hollywood Reporter*. "Well, Louella, it really is better for you if you don't write anything against me, for you see, I am Italian, and a mafioso, and I will cut your throat if you say anything about me that I don't like," I informed her over dinner. She started to shriek at the table when I said this, but she never dared write anything to embarrass or offend me. After twenty-seven years she still was convinced that if she did I would have her neck. She even invited me to her office, to keep me assured that she was on my side.

Katharine Hepburn

George Cukor and I did a lot of pictures together, and we were always friends. We had a lot in common, and enjoyed working together. For my screen test for my first picture, *A Bill of Divorcement*, he said that my acting was idiotic, but that I put a glass down brilliantly. We worked together for over forty years. The last projects were *Love Among the Ruins* with Larry Olivier and *The Corn Is Green*, which Bette had done in the forties. We did three with Spencer—*Keeper of the Flame*, *Adam's Rib*, and *Pat and Mike*—and three with Cary—*Sylvia Scarlett*, *Holiday*, and *The Philadelphia Story*—and *Little Women*, too.

Maureen O'Sullivan

I made *David Copperfield* under George Cukor in 1935. I didn't want to do that picture, and in fact tried to get out of it. I felt that I simply was not a wilting flower, just not at all right for a child bride. David Selznick made me stay on it, but I think George would agree with me that I was not right for the part. I recall reading an interview he gave in which he talked about how wonderful Madge Evans was in the film, and he didn't even mention me, so I suppose he thought I wasn't that good. I thought I was much more dashing than a child bride was supposed to be, and it's not pleasant to feel you're miscast. But then one can enjoy anything, if one wants to, and I did, for we had quite a cast: W.C. Fields, Freddie Bartholomew, Basil Rathbone, Lionel Barrymore, Elsa Lanchester, and quite a few others. I never got to know W.C. too well, since I would see him only coming in the door. "Good morning, my little chickadee," he would say to me as I was going out.

Audrey Hepburn

George Cukor was a very close friend of mine, too. *My Fair Lady* was my one and only occasion to work with him, but I adored him long before we ever did that picture together. He was one of the first people I met in Hollywood, in fact, for the great writer Anita Loos had given me a letter of introduction to him. She had done the English adaptation of *Gigi* for Colette, which I played on Broadway, long before the musical film version. I was invited to George's house, and we became great friends.

Maureen O'Sullivan

Whenever I came to Hollywood he was always the first person I called, and I really miss him. Once I was going to get married, and I just wasn't sure about it, so I asked George to come out to have dinner with me, to give me his opinion of the man. He refused, saying, "Why don't you come to dinner at my house? That would be a better way for me to give you my opinion of this man." So, my fiancé and I went, and he had Irene Selznick there, and Katharine Hepburn, and some other pretty sharp ladies. Well, the next morning he telephoned and said, "Don't marry him! He's too dull for you!" Well, I followed George's advice, and then married someone else. I just loved George. He was a real favorite of mine, and he's my daughter Mia's godfather, too.

Olivia de Havilland

I never knew how I was chosen to play Melanie in *Gone With the Wind* until I read *Memo*, this remarkable book put together by a chap with David O. Selznick's memoranda. In that book there is a memo that says that in the fall of 1938 David has seen *Robin Hood*, and thinks I'm the one he wants for Melanie. The memo says he wants to see how difficult it would be to get me for the part, since I was under contract to Warner Brothers. So, one day when I got back from location on *Dodge City*, up in Modesto, the phone rang, and it was George Cukor. Now my sister Joan in the meantime had seen George, since he had asked her to read for Melanie, but she had refused, since she didn't like the part, and wanted to play Scarlett. Apparently Joan said, "Well, if you want a Melanie, why don't you call my sister Olivia?" I brought this up to George many years later, and he said that nothing of the kind happened.

I had never met George before the phone rang that day, but of course I went to see all of his films, since he was a great director of Garbo. "Would you be interested in Melanie?" he asked. I said that I would, so he continued, "Would you mind coming and reading for me?" I said that I would be happy to, and then he warned me, "Of course, you have to keep it a secret." I said that I would, because what we were doing was illegal, since I was under contract to Warners.

I promised not to say a word to anyone, and he told me exactly where to come, so I met him in the afternoon at Selznick's. I think he gave me a scene from the book, and I read it. At the end he said, "I want to speak to David. I think he should see you." Then David told him to ask Miss de Havilland if she would come to the house on Sunday at three P.M. I said that I would be perfectly charmed to do so, so I got dressed and drove up there that Sunday. I was shown into a beautiful drawing room, with paneling and chintz, and in a few minutes George and David came in. Then George and I performed the scene, which I think he had told me to memorize, and I believe I did.

George played Scarlett to my Melanie, and it was an impassioned scene, with Selznick standing just a few paces away. I was thinking that this was absolutely lunatic, one of the most comical scenes ever performed, for George was very plump, with thick, black, curly hair, and heavy, dark, horn-rimmed spectacles. He was clutching the curtains with passion, and there I was, trying to play an equally passionate Melanie, thinking to myself, "How can anyone take this seriously?" I was wondering how I was going to keep a straight face, and keep my emotions straight, and play the scene seriously. I mean George was extremely plump, and he was playing Scarlett with passion!

Apparently I managed, though, because when it was over David said, "You are our Melanie." Then he did something very strange: he took George and me into the next room, where I met Irene Selznick. She was wearing a long hostess gown. They started to run all the tests of the different Melanies. I sat there, and I thought that they were all marvelous, especially Ann Sheridan. I realized that I had to restrain my enthusiasm, though, because I could really have influenced them to pick one of those other girls instead of me. I remember thinking to myself, "Why do they want me when they can have one of them?"

But they still wanted me, so after looking at all the tests they said, "Now we've got to do the very delicate operation of

persuading Jack Warner to let you go to us, and we know that
he's not known for cooperation with anyone." Well, those
negotiations did go on, and it was very delicate indeed. Finally
he let me go in exchange for Jimmy Stewart, who came over to
Warners in 1940 to do *No Time for Comedy* with Roz Russell.
So that was how I got to know George Cukor and played
Melanie in *Gone With the Wind*. I finally met Margaret Mitchell in Atlanta. We were all there for the premiere, and we
got a phone call that Miss Mitchell would receive us. We were
then dining, and she was to see us a little after nine P.M. It was
to be very hush-hush, and the press was not to know.

Katharine Hepburn

I never really knew David O. Selznick all that well, and I got
to know Irene, his wife, who was L. B. Mayer's daughter,
only after they had separated. We were always invited to
George Cukor's for dinner, and since we were always there we
always sat at the wrong end of the table, with the family, and
that's where we became friends, and have been ever since.
They all had great flair, but I didn't always approve of David.

Gregory Peck

I had a contract with Selznick also, for three pictures at least.
Only twice was I forced to make pictures I didn't want to do.
Once it was for Fox, after Zanuck had left and Spyros Skouras
had taken over. That was *Beloved Infidel*, in which I played F.
Scott Fitzgerald opposite Deborah Kerr. I said to them that I
didn't look anything like Scott Fitzgerald, and that people
knew what he looked like, so it would be a case of bad casting.
But they wanted me for the part, and they had a signed
commitment from me, so I had no choice. I finally said,
"Okay, but I'll look more like John Steinbeck than Scott
Fitzgerald. Can't you change the name of the character?"
They refused, and insisted that it had to go as planned, since it
was the autobiography of Sheilah Graham, the East End cock-

ney girl who rises to the dizzying heights of Hollywood gossip columnist, and they were going to use the real names. So, I did it, and I was named Scott Fitzgerald in the picture, but I didn't make any attempt at impersonation. I simply played it as an American writer. Incidentally, *Beloved Infidel* is a film I like, but a lot of people didn't. It broke a long cycle of very successful box office pictures that I made for Fox, since it went down the tubes.

Anyway, the other one I was forced to make was with Selznick, called *Only the Valiant*. Selznick's right-hand man, Danny O'Shea, called me up one day and said, "Greg, you've got to report to Warner Brothers because Bill Cagney, Jimmy's brother, has an independent unit, and they've got this Indian-fighting western to do. David has loaned you out to Warners." I was astonished, and said to him, "What do you mean? I haven't even read the script, and you're telling me to report on Monday? How can you send me over for costume fittings when I don't know anything about this project?" He asked me to come over to see him, so I did, and he sat me down and said, "David is broke, and he has a cash-flow problem. He gets you for $65,000, and now he has sold you for $150,000 to Warners. He feels embarrassed about it, and we all do, but he needs the cash that badly. You've got to do it."

I talked with my agent and my lawyer about it, and we thought about having a long-drawn-out court case, but they advised me to make the damned thing. It wasn't any good, just a picture about shooting Indians and defending the fort. I still have a lasting resentment over one thing about *Only the Valiant*: they didn't even make me a new cavalry uniform for it. They gave me stuff off the rack, and I recall climbing into a pair of cavalry pants, the blue ones with the yellow stripe up the side, and inside I saw a label. They had been Rod Cameron's old cavalry pants from another film. Now Rod was a nice guy, but all through the picture I thought to myself, "Goddammit, they wouldn't even make me a new pair of cavalry pants!" The picture went nowhere, of course.

Gina Lollobrigida

I met Selznick in 1954 when I made *Beat the Devil*, which was my first English-language movie. I remember that I accepted with joy the invitation to be with such big stars, including Humphrey Bogart, Jennifer Jones, and Robert Morley, and to be directed by John Huston. We shot the movie in Ravello. When I arrived David asked if I would withdraw my acceptance to do the picture, even though I had already signed the contract. I asked him why, and he offered to give me the money anyway, but I thanked him very much and said that I would do it anyway.

You see, Jennifer Jones had a starring role, and my part was very small, and in fact she was not jealous of me. It was Selznick trying to protect her, I think, for she was his wife at the time. She was a lovely lady. Truman Capote wrote the script, and he was there all the time, too, in order to watch out for his screenplay and to rewrite it as we went along. Every day he had to work on the script, and David made sure that he wrote good lines for Jennifer Jones. Actually, Truman wrote a lot of lines for me, too, because he liked me very much.

Robert Morley was a lot of fun, too, because he wanted to scare me, and at that time my English was very poor, so he would speak to me very sternly, as if he was angry with me. But he was not angry at all; he was just teasing me. By the end of the shooting, though, I understood his joke, so I decided to play the game on him. He was coproducing the movie with Humphrey and John, by the way. So, one day I suddenly began to act as if I was angry at him, and I stormed off the set, shouting in Italian, and he got terribly worried.

Every evening all the men would play as if they were fighting violently—Truman and Humphrey, as well as Huston and Morley, too. They would hit each other, and every morning Bogey would come down the steps with yet another Band-Aid on his face, singing as if nothing was wrong and with a big smile on his face.

The photographer Robert Capa was there with us, too,

Gina Lollobrigida, ca. 1982

and he played very roughly with the other men. In fact, one time he almost killed Huston. We were all playing Ping-Pong, and Capa hit the ball, but John missed it, so Capa hit him on the head with the paddle, and Huston almost collapsed. But in the case of all those fights at night, Truman was always the winner, believe it or not.

We had so much fun making that movie, but I remember that when the film came out it was a disaster. The producers were so afraid that it was going to flop that they had it open all over the United States at the same time, to evade the critics. But after ten years it was released again, and it became quite popular. I still think that *Beat the Devil* is among Truman's best work. It's such a shame that he let himself go at the end. I liked him a great deal. He was so much fun thirty-five years ago, but when I saw him the last time he wasn't even making any sense. Physically, too, he was another person at the end.

Olivia de Havilland

After *Gone With the Wind* was finished David came to me and discussed my doing *Rebecca*—quite seriously, too. I said that I would love to, since I had read the book, but then he found that it would be very difficult to get me back again from Warners. At the same time he had met my sister, and he wanted to put Joan under contract, so he was very straightforward with me. I said that I did not want to stand in her way, and that I would not. I thought that Joan was wonderful in *Rebecca*, and she should have gotten the Academy Award for that one, but she got it the next year for *Suspicion*. It was a big disappointment that she didn't win for *Rebecca*, though. I remember giving a little supper, for Mother, and Jimmy Stewart and Herbert Marshall, and Brian Aherne, who was then Joan's husband, but Joan didn't come to the party. It was before the premiere of *Rebecca*, and we all went to the opening of the film that night. She was stunning in that picture, and I was so happy that David had cast her.

Rossano Brazzi

As a matter of fact, I went to Hollywood because of David Selznick. I was already the number one star in Europe, and I really didn't want to go. Selznick was always trying to top his success in *Gone With the Wind*, so he came to Europe to persuade me to sign a contract with him. When I got to Hollywood I went to the Beverly Hills Hotel, and David got for me a villa on the corner of Rodeo Drive. It was number 708 North Rodeo Drive. Well, my wife started to cook, because otherwise we would have starved to death—the food available was just impossible. Then I got to know people who have been my close friends ever since: Ronald Reagan, Frank Sinatra, Dean Martin, and Sammy Davis.

Gregory Peck

It's true that in those days of the late forties Selznick was preoccupied with trying to top *Gone With the Wind*. Sometimes the stories were too small, and he should have been painting on a smaller canvas. I used to stop in his office for a Scotch with him before I went home after a day's shooting. He was always preparing for a night's work, to rewrite tomorrow's dialogue. He would send blue or brown or pink pages down to the set first thing every morning, so we all had to learn our new lines all over again. He would wear out about three secretaries each night, working until four A.M., and by the time we got in at seven A.M. the new pages of dialogue would be waiting. He was just compulsive in trying to outdo himself, which he never succeeded in doing. He could never do it bigger and better, no matter how hard he tried. *Gone With the Wind* still looks great today. I remember asking David one time, "Why don't you just make a nice little picture about some kids on a park bench talking about their problems?" He answered, "I can't! Don't you understand? I made *Gone With the Wind* when I was thirty-nine, and I already know what my obituary is going to say, and I can't stand it! I've got to top myself!" Picture-making was his life, and he just ate it up. He really loved it. He was like a big kid with a great toy. He really had a penchant for the overblown, too.

One of those big films of his from the period was *Duel in the Sun*, which was an outrageous, melodramatic, satirical western. We knew what we were doing, and that it verged on parody. The trick was to play it just straight enough that it didn't lose credibility. We all played it as a kind of poker-faced comedy, Lionel Barrymore and Lillian Gish and Joe Cotten and Jennifer Jones. We were definitely on the edge there, in this steamy, sex-laden, Selznick western. It was almost Oriental, just terribly lavish. No saloon in the history of the Old West ever existed like the one we had in that film, with hundreds of buckaroos crowded around the circular bar where Tillie Losch danced.

Actually, David was there on the set of *Duel in the Sun* when Jennifer Jones—whom he had not yet married in 1947—and I were shooting at each other at the end. We couldn't stand to be apart, and we couldn't stand to be together, so we ended up killing each other. David was actually out there on the set with a bucket of blood, splashing us.

One day he got so excited that he started to direct Jennifer and Charlie Bickford over King Vidor's shoulder. Now King Vidor was a pretty strong director. "No, no, Charlie, put a little more passion into it," David was saying in his enthusiasm, and then, "King, is it all right if we shoot that one scene again?" Well, King got very slowly up from his chair, out in the middle of the desert outside of Tucson. It had been building up to this, since David's enthusiasm was just spilling over, so King put on his leather jacket, picked up his script, and turned around toward Selznick. "David," he said, "take this picture and shove it up your ass!" Then he walked off the long distance to his Cadillac, parked with all the other Cadillacs and buses, and he got in. We all stood there and watched him drive off to the horizon. Finally Selznick said, "Well, I guess I must have said something wrong."

That led to the shutting down of production for a few days, and then we got William Dieterle as the new director. He was kind of a colorful Germanic type who always wore white cotton gloves, and was always well dressed. He had a certain European curl to his hat, and I think he was a good director. I think he ended up directing about a third of the film, because King never did come back; he meant what he said.

You know, you can get so wrapped up in these projects that the movie starts to seem like the whole world to you, as if "only this movie is happening" and everything else is unimportant. For example, on *The Big Country*, about ten years later, I was the star as well as the coproducer, and I had been working on it for about a year prior to filming. We never did get a script we were satisfied with, by the way. There were actually times on the set when I was scribbling lines on a yellow pad, which I would then hand to Willie Wyler, who was directing *The Big Country*. I would quickly write six alternate lines for Charlton Heston to say, and Willie would take his choice, then say, "Chuck, try this out!" He would do that with Jean Simmons and Carroll Baker and Burl Ives, too. We had been through seven writers, and it was rough going.

So, there was this occasion when I thought I deserved a retake. It was a little scene in a horse-drawn buckboard. There was something in the way I behaved or moved that I knew was wrong. I felt that I looked like an absolute cretin up there, and I couldn't bear the thought that this shot was going to be in the picture. I kept saying to Willie while we were still out there with the horses and buckboard and Carroll, "Let's do a little retake on that scene." Well, he would nod and ignore me, and finally it got to be the last day before we packed everything up to leave the location. "Willie, it's the last day, and I've just got to do a retake of that scene," I insisted. "It's nagging at me and driving me crazy." "Well, I'm not going to do it," he announced, "and I'm tired of hearing you talk about it, and I'll find a way to cut around it." He was clearly irritated, too.

To my own astonishment, I went to my Winnebago, got out of my western suit, got into my car, and drove all the way to Los Angeles, which was about four hundred miles away. My wife was so surprised to see me at home when I pulled in late that night. "What are you doing here?" she demanded to know. "Well, I walked off the set," I informed her. "But it's your own set," she reminded me. "How can you walk off your own set?" "I don't know," I admitted, "but it just seemed like the right thing to do." I explained to her that I felt I deserved that retake. I guess it shows you how tunnel-visioned you can become.

Willie and I were the best of friends before that, and we didn't even speak for about three years after this dispute, and I finished the picture with him not directing me. I was right there in front of him playing scenes, and had not one word from him, with only about a week to go. Our wives were very good friends, too, and not a single word for three years. I loved Willie. The upshot of it all was that he won the Oscar for directing *Ben-Hur*, and I was the next presenter in the wings, where I thought to myself, "This is the time." This little guy whom I loved was walking toward me with his Oscar, and so I said, "Willie, congratulations! You surely deserved it!" And he said, "Thanks, but I'm still not going to retake the buckboard scene!" That was the end of the feud. We loved each other again, and saw one another regularly until he died.

Geraldine Fitzgerald

Willie Wyler was very difficult to work with. When we were shooting *Wuthering Heights* he used to sit under the camera in the morning and say to us—by "us" I mean Laurence Olivier, Merle Oberon, Flora Robson, Donald Crisp, David Niven, and myself—"Show me what you're going to do." We would proceed to do so, and then he would say, "That's awful! Do something else!" So, we would figure out what we were going to do, while he would take up his newspaper and bury himself in it. When we were ready he would put down his newspaper and look at what we had to show him. "That's even worse!" he would say, and this would go on every day. Finally, after about an hour of this Willie would say, "Well, let's just shoot the first one you did, even though it wasn't very good." And we would shoot the first one, even though by that point we had no idea what the first one was. And then he would do fifty takes, and then not know which one to use.

His genius was that he could distill you—the way you would distill wine into brandy, I guess. He could tell when you were at your peak, and that was the one he would keep. I think that he was without any question the greatest director I ever had, and Larry Olivier thought so, too. We all forgave Willie for his tyranny when *Wuthering Heights* came out, too, for we all felt proud to be a part of it. In fact, I was nominated for the Oscar for my work in it, thanks to him.

I happened to see it again last summer on a boat, and it had the same power and pull. It had such a poetic feeling of danger, such an evocative atmosphere, almost scary, with a breathless quality. It's still a very touching picture, and every time I see it it makes me cry. The thing I remember best about that film is that David Niven refused to cry at the death of Cathy. He was commanded to cry by Willie—who did "command" us, by the way. He would say, "Now cry, David," and David would say, "No, I'm not going to." Willie would glare back at him and say, "Yes, you will. You're going to cry because I've asked you to." Then David surprised us all by saying, "It's in my contract that I don't have to cry in any film I'm in!" Willie replied with "That's ridiculous! No such contract was ever written!" "Okay," David rejoined, "send to the front office for my contract." Willie did, and when it came back he read it, and sure enough it said: "Mr. Niven will not be required to cry." So David got his way. I think that often enough he did cry, if he wasn't asked to, but he was very firm about this special clause. Willie just gave up on making David cry and told him to bury his head in the bedclothes instead, which he did, and it proved to be very moving.

Gregory Peck

David Niven was quite extraordinary. He's one of the three people Véronique and I miss the most. People are dying like flies around here, including all of my old friends. We really haven't gotten used to the idea that Cary is gone, but the ones apart from him whom we miss the most are Jack Benny, Rosalind Russell, and David Niven. All of them were so genuinely sweet and funny and unspoiled and entertaining. They were all very caring people, and would have been re-markable no matter what line of work they had entered.

Loretta Young

David Niven lived with our family for about a year when he was just starting out in Hollywood in 1934. I think he had a crush on each one of us, starting with Mama, who just took him under her wing. Then he became interested in Polly Ann, but then she started going with someone else, so he moved on to Sally, but she also found a steady, and then he came to me.

Sally had invited him for a weekend after meeting him in England, so he became like a member of the family. The two boys he came with left on Monday, but David had no job, so he just stayed on with us when Mama invited him to. After all, we had the guest room free. I was delighted, though there were of course times when we all wondered when that guy was going to leave, because it had been a houseful of women, and suddenly with a man on the premises you had to start watch-ing how you walked around undressed.

David was always very sweet and dear, but I never had any crush on him, though oddly enough I played his wife much later in *The Bishop's Wife*.

Audrey Hepburn

I met David Niven at the time I was playing *Gigi* on Broad-way. He was playing in *Nina* with Gloria Swanson, and we were all staying in the Blackstone hotel. While we were living there someone threw himself out one of the windows, in fact. That caused quite a sensation at the hotel. We had quite a collection there, for Sarah Churchill Beauchamp was residing there at the same time. I didn't get to meet Gloria Swanson then, but I did much later on, because I had become great friends with her daughter, who was engaged to and subsequently married the producer of the film I had made in Monte Carlo, *Monte Carlo Baby*.

Helen Hayes

The last picture I did, about ten years ago, starred David Niven, whom I adored. It was called *Candleshoe*, and one day on the set David showed me a letter that he had just received from Marlene Dietrich, in which she wrote: "Thank you so much for what you have said about me in your latest interview." Apparently she had a clipping service that sent her everything that appeared about her, and she read it all, which shows you that she was still very much interested in and aware of the world of show business. She went on to say that people seemed to want to portray her as an ignorant fool in the things they wrote about her, and that it not only hurt her feelings, but was untrue.

I asked David what he had been asked in the interview that led him to speak of Marlene, and he said, "Who was the actress who would make the most satisfying lover?" David told me that his answer was: "The sexiest woman I have ever known was undoubtedly Marlene Dietrich, but she was never my mistress, sadly enough. I say that not simply because of her great beauty, but also because of her intelligence." That made her happy.

Douglas Fairbanks, Jr.

One time my wife and I were taking a trip through the Mediterranean, and David Niven was filming something close

Douglas Fairbanks, Jr., ca. 1928

by with Otto Preminger, so he came over for lunch. Now David was terrified of Otto, so when he came by he was shaking, trembling with fear, and stammering. "What do I do, Douglas?" he was cringing to me. "I've never worked with anyone like this! I can't go on! What do I do about this maniac?" He was really shaking like a leaf, so I said, "Why, you have to maniac back at him, of course."

The only time I ever walked off a movie set was due to Otto's awful behavior. He had yelled and screamed and insulted an electrician, who didn't dare answer back. I spoke up for the guy and told Otto that it was not his fault, saying, "You must apologize to him just as prominently as you have bawled him out." "No, I will do no such thing!" he raged. "Oh, yes you will, Otto," I insisted, "or I will walk off this set and shut down this production. You mustn't take advantage of your position to abuse these people." "Oh, don't be silly, Douglas, please," he begged me, but I went home, telling him to phone me after he had apologized to the guy, which he soon did.

Gregory Peck

David Niven was one of the most naturally charming and sophisticated gentlemen ever to act in films, and much more. *The Sea Wolves* was the last picture we made together, but I had known David very well since making *The Guns of Navarone* twenty years earlier, in 1960. That one was a serious war drama, to all intents and purposes, but we played it like a straight-faced comedy, since we accomplished such incredible things in it. Basically, six men beat up on the whole German army, which is not too realistic, in a Keystone Cops style. Every time they chased us it was like a Buster Keaton sequence, and that's how we got away with all those heroics, just on the edge of parody. In a sense, you play it like a comedy, but you don't let them know that it's being played like a comedy. It's the attitude you strike toward the material. It proved to be a very entertaining, effective movie, nudging against the satirical, where a band of intrepid commandos saves part of the British fleet by blowing up these gigantic German guns that cover an outlet to the sea.

The Sea Wolves was about a bunch of overage former military men who organize themselves into a commando troop to put a German ship anchored in the harbor of neutral Goa out of commission. A military mission would violate Portuguese neutrality, so it has to be accomplished otherwise. Now at the time we made *The Sea Wolves*, I noticed that David was doing things that worried me, although he never said that anything was wrong. He was very religious about taking long, brisk walks, and this fixation on exercise was new to me. It really had never before been a part of his life. Then I realized that his speech was sounding cloudy, and he looked a little thin. But he never complained.

Then one time he came out here to make a speech about a director for whom he had worked, and his speech was even more clouded, and everyone at this American Film Institute tribute noticed it. Finally it came out that he had Lou Gehrig's disease. He and I used to correspond quite a lot, and he would write about his taking long walks out among the Grand Cap pines beside our old house on the Riviera. I was very worried about him, and indeed all of his friends were, for he was getting much worse.

The last communication I had with him was when I was in Hong Kong, where I had gone to see producer Run Run Shaw and to visit his studio, where I watched them shoot those karate and kung fu films that are so popular all over the Far East, though God knows why. Anyway, we went into Run Run Shaw's office, and he brought out a mahogany or teak-wood box, highly polished, which he opened. It was lined with red velvet, and lying inside was a strange thing: ginseng root. It was the part that grows underground, beneath this sprig of green shrubbery on top, and it had come from the mountains of mainland China. It's a bit like truffles: hard to find. These mountaineers would dig them out with little spoons so that the entire root would be preserved intact. It has a strange look to it also, at first glance almost like a human skeleton.

What they believe is that when it is ground up it does everything for you. Run Run Shaw was about seventy at that time—and a very charming fellow, I might add, and fabulously rich—and he said, "Gregory, I take three capsules of this every morning, and three more each night before I go to bed. I have a man grind this root up for me into a powder. I wash it down with a tot of Scotch, and I can still do everything—*everything*—that I could do when I was thirty." He winked with that certain grin to make sure I knew what he meant by "everything." He seemed to be surrounded by smiling secretaries and smiling starlets, so I got the picture. "I can do it just as well as I could forty years ago," he assured me.

So, I got the idea that some of this ginseng might somehow help David, and I bought some. It was very costly, too. I sent it to David and asked him to try it. "Who knows?" I wrote, "They claim it's good for everything." Well, there was a letter waiting for me when I got back, and it was David's last letter. It said, "The doctors control my intake of everything, and they won't let me have it. I'm on a very special diet of vegetables and herbs. I'd like to try it, but they won't let me. I've been to every quack in Europe, and have even been to see a fellow in a place called Dion. He immersed me in olive oil, in a tub of it, and then kneaded me like dough until I squealed in pain. I have to admit that I felt pretty good after this faith healer finished with me, but it lasted only about three hours. This farmer had hands like a bunch of bananas, and he rubbed me while saying a bunch of mumbo jumbo." He was very poetic in that last letter, talking about those long walks, and looking at the cliffs along the coast toward Monte Carlo, behind which he could see the snow on the French Alps.

Katharine Hepburn

You can't make people have any sense about death. It really depresses them. I believe that we go into the ground in comfort, which must be a great relief.

Bette Davis

Miss Hepburn and I should each thank our Yankee ancestors that we're both still around. Yankees live forever, you know. I have met many of them who are still walking around at one hundred or even one hundred ten years of age.

Douglas Fairbanks, Jr.

The trouble with dying these days is that once you're gone they try to tear you apart. "The evil that men do lives after them, the good is oft interred with their bones." That's from *Julius Caesar*, by the way. These daughters of Joan Crawford and Bette Davis have certainly tried to fix their mothers. There are all kinds of actors and actresses, just as there are all kinds of doctors and dentists, bankers and lawyers. They are not all monsters.

When I was a precocious teenager writing poetry I envisioned myself as a Shelley or Byron or Keats, and I felt that I would die by the age of twenty-three. So, I decided to cram as much living and experience into my life as I could, and when I reached twenty-three I thought that I would make it to twenty-four, so I kept on crowding things in. I don't really know what motivated me, other than curiosity, for I've always been very curious about everything. I've never been bored, and I'm very intolerant of people who are bored. Perhaps that's a drawback, since there may be people who are dedicated to a certain job, and who are bored by everything else, but who are not boring in themselves. I don't know. But I'm still just as voracious, and I'm over eighty.

Rossano Brazzi

Sometimes I awake in the middle of the night and think to myself, "What is going on? Am I now forty-five? No, I remember being fifty-five. But then I can recall my sixty-fifth birthday. Oh, my God, I am over seventy years old!" That scares me. I can still play tennis well enough for three hours to beat the kids who are twenty years old. I played sports all my life, and might have won a gold medal at the Olympics, but age is catching up with me. Last year I got a call from the big impresario Bruno Campioni, who brought Frank Sinatra to Italy, and he wanted me to introduce some of my old friends from Hollywood at an awards presentation. They were Robert Mitchum, who was then about seventy, and Joseph Cotten, who was then maybe eighty-three, and Bette Davis, who was then eighty, and June Allyson, who is also about seventy. I know because I made two pictures with her, *Little Women* and *Interlude*. The fifth one was Glenn Ford, whom I will always remember as the man who made *Gilda* with Rita Hayworth. He was then in his early seventies, so when you added up all of our ages you got about five hundred.

Gina Lollobrigida

You know, at my home in Rome I have a corridor lined with photos of all of my leading men from all of the movies I have made. On one side I keep the pictures of all the actors who are still alive, like Sean Connery and Burt Lancaster and Jean-Paul Belmondo, and on the other wall I keep those who have died, like Humphrey Bogart, and Errol Flynn, and James Mason, and Tyrone Power, and Ralph Richardson, and Peter Lawford. It scares me to see that I keep moving the souvenir pictures of my costars from the right wall to the left. They're all dying off.

George C. Scott

This morning I was watching *Fort Apache* with Henry Fonda and John Wayne. I counted all of them, and said to my wife Trish, "Everyone in this picture is dead, except Shirley Temple, who has not been too well, and her ex-husband John Agar." Duke; Fonda; Victor McLaglen, whom I adored;

Ward Bond, whom I loved; George O'Brien; Dick Foran; Pedro Armendariz, who killed himself. It was like a roll call of the dead.

James Stewart

Henry Fonda was one of my closest friends for nearly sixty years. He was several years older than I. At Princeton I had decided that my field was going to be architecture. It was the day of commencement, and I was walking across the campus to get my diploma, a bachelor of science in architecture, when my classmate, Josh Logan, came up to me. "I know that you're an architect," he said to me, "but why don't you take the summer off and come up to Cape Cod to join a little acting company we've put together?" I had already been awarded a scholarship to get my master's in architecture, and I thought that my life was not only planned, but on track. "We have a theater up in Falmouth, Massachusetts, and we call ourselves the University Players. It would be a nice summer for you, at the seashore in the company of a lot of people you know, and we would give you plenty of good parts. You could even play your accordion in the tea room if you like," he offered, trying his best to persuade me to join up with him as an actor.

Actually, I've talked to Josh several times over the years about this, at tributes to him and elsewhere, and I told him that if it hadn't been for his walking across the campus that spring morning I would either have been an architect or ended up working in my father's hardware store in Indiana, Pennsylvania. Henry also took up with one of these summer stock or strawhat companies on Cape Cod, and he had done that for several summers, as had Margaret Sullavan. I didn't work with Fonda at that time, though he visited our outfit.

Later on, when we all decided to become actors on Broadway, we shared a small apartment on West 63rd Street, back in the early thirties. Actually, there were quite a few of us in that apartment—Myron McCormick, who was in my class at

Henry Fonda, ca. 1935

Princeton; and Dick Foran, who also graduated from Princeton; and Kent Smith, who was a Harvard man. All of us came out here to make movies. Anyway, we were all in there together, and we all wanted to be in the movies. It was a very small two-room apartment, with a tiny kitchen. Whoever was working paid for the food, and sometimes the rent, which was about forty-five dollars a week.

The gangster Legs Diamond owned the building, by the way, but we had no idea until one night when we were all sitting around talking and a key went into the door. No one had buzzed, but suddenly the door opened and four men came in. They marched in single file in derby hats and stopped in front of us. Well, we sat there silently looking at them, and then one of them turned to their boss and said, "We must be on the wrong floor, sir. I'm sorry." Then they walked out without ever saying a word to us, so we began to suspect that there was something going on, and we soon discovered that our landlord was Legs Diamond.

Anyway, it was in that period in New York that Henry and I became friends. I still think of him as a very loyal and close friend, with tremendous energy and a total love of theater and of acting. He did everything very quietly, and with great modesty, a true gentleman. He believed in hard work, and he kept at it as long as he could. It was a wonderful influence on me, too, to see him apply this constant effort to his craft. I learned a great deal from watching him work. We learned from one another, I guess.

Bette Davis

I had met Henry Fonda many years ago at the Cape Cod Playhouse. He was a young actor there when I was doing plays back in the late twenties. He was certainly a very nice person, too, and in my view he eventually became a very great actor. He was wonderful to work with in *Jezebel*, too. Some of the things he did later in the theater, like *Clarence Darrow*, which came much later in his career, were superb.

James Stewart

When Henry and I double-dated with Ginger Rogers and Lucille Ball in the late thirties we would hit the Trocadero first, and then go to the Mocambo for breakfast. It was a transformed railroad car down on Doheny, and it was still standing until only a year or so ago. But the Trocadero was the place we all went. Every Saturday night it was jam-packed to the rafters, mostly with young movie people like myself, and we could dance until five in the morning. I had such a great time there, as we all did. Jack Benny would get up in front of Phil Harris' orchestra and tell a number of jokes, and then there would be a crack from behind him in the middle of one of his jokes, and down would come George Burns. Then Jack would move off and George would tell his jokes.

I will never forget one time when a middle-aged woman walked up and tapped Phil Harris on the shoulder, and then whispered something to him. Then Phil turned around and announced to the audience that this woman had brought her daughter down to the Trocadero after signing a contract with MGM. "Her mother wants her to get used to singing in front of an audience," he continued, "so I want to ask you people who are here tonight what you think about that." Well, the response was about half and half, but Phil let her go on anyway, dressed in bobby sox. The little girl turned out to be Judy Garland, and she sang for half an hour. Needless to say, Judy was just wonderful. It was a great way to wind up a long week of work, for you were busy all the time, with these ten-hour days making pictures. Saturday night you got to play, and then Sunday you rested up to get ready to go back to work early Monday morning. It was truly a wonderful life back then, for the partying was fun, but so was the working, and all of us were busy all the time.

Maureen O'Sullivan

I did *Let Us Live* with Henry Fonda in 1937 for Columbia, and I have to say that he was just wonderful looking. And so quiet. He kept to himself all the time, but then most of my scenes were with Ralph Bellamy. I liked Fonda very much.

Katharine Hepburn

Henry was great fun to work with when we made *On Golden Pond*, and I thought he was very funny, and very true. That picture was apparently of fundamental interest to people.

Loretta Young

I made *Alexander Graham Bell* with Henry in 1939 for Fox, and sadly I hardly got to know him at all at the time. Personally I saw more of him "out," but not as a date. I found him charming, too.

Once I was starting a youth group down in Arizona, and he came down with something about Abraham Lincoln. I was staying with a group of nuns in their convent, so when he came to town I asked these sisters how they would like to go to see Henry Fonda on the stage as Abe Lincoln. Well, they all wanted to go, and I said that I could take only four of them, so they chose among themselves who would go. Then I called up the manager, and he was delighted to be able to tell everyone that Loretta Young was coming.

Well, I tell you there were enough four-letter words in that play to shake your teeth out, and here I had brought these four little nuns, and they were sitting there smiling impassively, with a glazed expression. After the play I asked them if they would like to go backstage to meet Mr. Fonda, which of course they wanted to do. The manager came to get us and said that he would go first, since all the cast members were men, and they often ran around undressed. I asked him to warn them that there were five women coming backstage, so as we proceeded toward Henry's dressing room all the doors began to slam shut. Henry leaned out of his door, and said, "Oh, my God, you didn't bring four nuns to this play?!" "Yes, I did, and here we are," I returned. He had us come into his dressing room, where he offered us sherry, and he told us how embarrassed he was. I said that the nuns knew all the words, even though they didn't use them, and that he should not worry about it. Hank was a very sensitive man whom I liked a great deal, and I liked his wife Shirlee, too. I did not get to know his previous wife Frances Brokaw very well.

Audrey Hepburn

Henry Fonda was also a dear friend of mine for many years, and my husband Mel Ferrer had been friends with him for many years before that. Mel wanted Henry for the role of Pierre in *War and Peace*, and that was not an easy picture to make. It was all done in Rome, since Dino De Laurentiis was producing it, in conjunction with Carlo Ponti, who was not yet married to Sophia Loren. This was in 1956. King Vidor, another master of the craft, was the director of that epic. *War and Peace* was possibly the hardest to do of all the pictures that I made. As is typical of such huge projects, especially international coproductions, there were unexpected problems. We were in the middle of shooting it in August, and in Rome at that time of year you can hardly function in the heat and humidity. On top of that we were dressed in furs and heavy gowns, so you can imagine the difficulty of filming those enormous battle scenes, like Borodino, in that kind of heat. And yet we made it, thanks in large part to King Vidor's determination. When directors are good they tend to have a lot in common.

James Stewart

Hank Fonda was a practicing Democrat, and "to the left," I suppose you would say. Years and years ago, back when we were living in New York, we had gotten into a terrible fight about our differing political views. In fact, we could never talk about politics without getting mad at each other, so one day in

James Stewart, ca. 1937

a bar I said to him, "Why don't we just agree never to talk politics again, in order to avoid arguments like this?" And he said to me, "I'll buy that." That was the last time we ever mentioned it, and we remained the best of friends for the next fifty years. Fonda was quite liberal, and his daughter Jane has done a number of things over the years that people have questioned. But Henry never went against her. He stayed behind her and supported Jane in all of her protests. I admired him for that, even though I never agreed with the positions she was taking.

Olivia de Havilland

When Henry and I worked together he was very happily married with two children, and they would come and visit on the set of *The Male Animal* in 1942. I can remember being with Jimmy Stewart one night, and Henry's wife, Frances, had just had a baby, and it must have been Peter. Jane must have come in and said something. I really didn't get to know Henry well then, but I did later on when we did a play together. That was *A Gift of Time*, and then I really did admire him. He was really quite different from Jimmy, contrary to opinion, for they were not the same fellow at all. Henry was much more intellectual than Jimmy. Henry was very intelligent, which is not to say that Jimmy isn't, but in a different way. Henry was very keen, and a pro, and very fair. He wanted everybody to be good, and that's the best idea of all.

He was a wonderful actor, and wanted everyone else to do his or her best. I respected that so much, and he was always looking out for me, too. One time we were trying a play out in Philadelphia, and he said to me, "I would like to see you sometime tomorrow," and I said, "Well, what for?" "I would like to discuss your performance with you," he replied. "You would?" I answered, very perplexed, and he nodded. I thought about that, and then responded with "What about eleven o'clock in the morning, before we go on for the mati-

nee?" I was staying in the bridal suite in a hotel on Ritten-
house Square, and he said that that would be agreeable to
him. He presented himself at the door to my suite at the
appointed hour, and I greeted him with "Well, Henry, you
wanted to discuss my performance with me, so what is it that
you want to say?" He leaned on the mantelpiece and said, "I
have six criticisms of your work to convey to you."

Then he started off with "Now in this scene . . ." and he
told me what I was doing wrong. "And in that scene . . ." and
he kept on until he had given me six different points. Well, I
was outraged, but I was sobered, because I had a feeling that
there was a certain amount of sense to what he was saying, and
that made me even madder. That made me *really* angry. But I
did have a lot of respect for him, so I said, "Well, Henry, I see
what you mean. We have a matinee this afternoon, so I will try
to get into the performance three of your suggestions, so you
can judge if you think they improve the play, and in the
evening performance I will try to get in three more. If I fail I
will try again tomorrow."

Well, that afternoon I got in five of the six, and I realized
as I was playing the scenes that he was absolutely right. I was
really upset, and I kicked the door between our two dressing
rooms I was so mad. I nearly broke my toe doing it, too!
"Dammit, you are right! You're right! How can you be so
right?" I shouted at him when I got back to my dressing
room, and started kicking. "How can you be such an S.O.B.?
But you are right!" He never knew that this scene was going
on on the other side of the door, I'm sure. That night I got the
sixth one in and it made all the difference. He was simply
perfect in his performance, too.

I saw his performance as *Mister Roberts* on Broadway, too,
and I never got over it. Oh, what a performance that was!
Much much later my daughter Giselle insisted on taking me to
see *On Golden Pond*, when I was to leave Paris the next day for
the United States to make a film, and I said, "But darling,
really. I've got to pack and to get myself ready." But she
wouldn't hear any of that, so she and a friend took me to see

that terribly moving film, and then to supper. I was up until two o'clock in the morning, and then took the plane that day.

The most extraordinary thing was that just after I had completed the assignment, whatever that film was, and I had my bags packed to leave for Paris, the phone rang. It was NBC or CBS, and they said, "Have you heard the news?" I asked what news they meant, and they told me that Henry Fonda was gone. They asked me to please say a few words, for they were going to book me onto "Good Morning America," or whatever show it was. It meant that I had to be at the studio at four-thirty in the morning.

"Will you do this? We would like to gather together Henry Fonda's friends out here to talk about him, and devote the whole program to him," they told me. I was all packed and supposed to leave on the plane that night, but I told them that I would put it off, which I did. I didn't have anything suitable to wear, since I wanted to look sober, so I got a navy-blue dress. I thought that that would be appropriate, and that Henry would have expected that, a dark dress. So, I got up at that early hour, and spoke about him, and it was indeed a great loss. He was wonderful in *On Golden Pond*, and I was able to speak about it because I had seen it, thanks to Giselle. The beginning of that trip was *On Golden Pond*, and the end of it was Henry's going.

Scene Five

Entrée

As the clock strikes eight the Royals contemplate Olivia de Havilland's moving recollection of Fonda. Silently, the waiters wheel the tremendous tureen out and roll in yet another caravan of enormous trolleys, though there is still no sign of Mr. Hearst. Could it be that his global publishing empire is requiring his sudden attention? Perhaps some new mining or lumber project demands diplomatic persuasion, or possibly the government has called upon his influence to avert a war. Maybe he has been presented with a project for Marion Davies, who might want to star in a new epic.

In any event, the host has not arrived in time for the main course of this extravagant feast, but the show must go on. After all, his guests reason, perhaps he never intended to make a personal appearance at this festive soirée, preferring simply to cast the movie, to leave the script to the actors themselves, and to let the butler direct the flow of action according to the menu.

With Jimmy Stewart seated at the northern end of the long table, flanked by a glowing Katharine Hepburn on his right and a bejeweled Bette Davis on his left, the constellation of stars lights up the room from one end to the other, where Gregory Peck is holding court between the sensuous Ava Gardner to his right and a serene Audrey Hepburn to his left. While the staff of waiters serve them the filet mignon, the lobster, and the swan, the conversation is renewed by the ever-resourceful Jack Lemmon. He deftly picks up the threads of thought and continues the Henry Fonda stories with *Mister Roberts*, in which they costarred with James Cagney.

This leads Cagney himself to recall the good old days, and Lauren Bacall to remember her late husband Humphrey Bogart. *Casablanca* soon follows, as does Ingrid Bergman, whose romance with Roberto Rossellini leads to European gossip. Sultry Gina Lollobrigida and dashing Marcello Mastroianni contribute tales of Federico Fellini and Sophia Loren, whose costar in *Timbuktu*, John Wayne, concludes this course of the dinner party.

Jack Lemmon

Mister Roberts was only my fourth film, but by that time I had already fallen deeply in love with making movies. Working with big pros like Henry Fonda and Jimmy Cagney and Bill Powell was just extraordinary for me. I assure you that it is not the norm for the biggest stars to be such wonderful people. I stayed close to every one of those gentlemen, right up to the end. All of them were extraordinary men.

Hank Fonda, for example, was very much in person as he came across on the screen. He was as strong as a rock, just filled with leadership qualities. He instilled a great deal of faith in everyone working with him. As an actor you realized even more how much he was doing in a given scene, standing like the Rock of Gibraltar for the other actors. He was just superb. He also had a wonderful sense of humor, which he did not very often get a chance to show in his work. He was such a compassionate and sensitive man. I was very attracted to the way he thought and felt about things. I believe that there is a tendency to want to extol someone who thinks the way you do, to like that person for that reason, but in Henry's case it went far beyond that. His humanity was immense and profound. His concern about specific causes was heartfelt, and his attitude about issues in the arts, particularly the theater, was special. He felt that the stage was a hallowed place, and he approached it that way. He was truly a dedicated professional who cared very genuinely about many things. If he supported something, then it was all the way. He had a remarkable talent, and he was always quiet about it, which is a rare quality that came across in all that he did on the screen. He had a rather silent kind of strength, and in a way he was quite modest. Apart from his gifts as an actor he painted up a storm, too!

Actually, Jimmy Cagney was a fine painter as well. One of the things I treasure most is a pair of still lifes that Cagney did back-to-back for me. We had to put it into a frame that you can turn, since there is a painting on each side. The subjects of them are flowers—just the very opposite of what you might expect of Jimmy. On top of that he wrote poetry, beautiful verses, almost like wisps of smoke, just wonderfully ethereal lines. Like Fonda, Cagney was a total pro, and he worked hard during the making of *Mister Roberts*.

Nonetheless, the two of them approached the work completely differently. Jimmy's attitude about it all was remarkable, for he seemed to view the work as something that afforded him the ability to concentrate on other things. To a great extent he loved performing, but he also loved other activities, which he was then able to pursue because of his work in films. In addition to painting and poetry he adored horse breeding and sailing. He actually became an expert on soil conservation and treatment, and he wrote papers about what he had discovered. He even went to Washington to assist Rachel Carson on ecological matters. He had antennae out for everything. Jimmy is an extraordinarily bright man, too, which is perhaps not so well known.

All three of them exemplify something special, I think, and it is not obvious just to me. I have lived too long and worked with too many good actors to be mistaken about this, for whatever it is that constitutes talent, creative and interpretive, all three of them were exceptionally intelligent men. In fact, I have never known a good actor who was really dumb. Certain ones may seem it, and even behave as if they are dim-witted, not to mention a pain in the ass and a two-year-old child, but that doesn't mean they are dumb. The perception and sensitivity needed to go through the mental process of observing human behavior beyond what the normal person must do is a fundamental part of intelligence. I believe that sensitivity and intelligence are intertwined or overlapped to that extent, for a great deal of acting is a mental process.

The great part of making *Mister Roberts* was that each of those three men was exactly as he seemed to be. For instance, Bill Powell was every bit as urbane as he appeared to be in *The Thin Man*, and everywhere else he acted. He became sort of the den papa of our group, and every time I saw him I found myself smiling.

We were all living in the bachelor officers' quarters on Midway Island, which is just a bloody sandbar that had a chance and took it. It is without a doubt the dullest place on earth. So, Bill set up a two-bit café for us, and whenever he wasn't filming a scene he'd be bustling around, cleaning it up and keeping it neat. I can recall his commandeering Ritz crackers and peanut butter and even a little bit of jelly for us, and he kept the bar stocked. If Bill hadn't been shooting with us then we would find him behind the bar when we came back from the set. He would always be wearing his underwear, his boxer shorts, with a pair of fuzzy slippers, which were not as common back in 1955 as they are now. It was quite a sight.

It was mighty hot on Midway, so that's all he would be wearing. But I would look at him and I could swear that he was wearing a tuxedo. He had that rare ability to appear so sophisticated, no matter what the circumstances. He was just the most charming, wonderful man, and even if he had on only a jockstrap he would seem elegant.

Maureen O'Sullivan

I appeared in *The Thin Man* with William Powell and Myrna Loy, and that was the first time they worked together. At first Bill wasn't quite used to Myrna. She is rather shy, apart from

Maureen O'Sullivan, ca. 1930

being perfectly adorable and a joy to work with. Since Myrna was somewhat withdrawn, Bill used to take me out instead of his leading lady. We would go to his house and swim between takes. Of course, they went on to do a number of other films in *The Thin Man* series, but I appeared only in the original one, so he kind of forgot about me. Later I asked him how he was getting along with Myrna, and he said, "Oh, Myrna, she's just divine!" They were a very accomplished screen team, and he could mix a martini like no one else.

Jack Lemmon

He had come out of retirement to make *Mister Roberts*, and he had already had the first colostomy. I remember that during the first two weeks he was very trepidatious about it all. You could look down between takes and see that his hand was shaking. Now Bill was a seasoned star who knew film inside out, so perhaps it was just the idea of coming back that unnerved him a bit. It proved to be his last film, too, though he lived for many years after it. But Bill wanted so badly to do that picture with Hank and Jimmy and John Ford. Of course, he was marvelous in it, as were Hank and Jimmy, and thanks to them I got my first Oscar for it.

James Cagney

Making *Mister Roberts* offered me the chance to visit the South Pacific, but it also meant working under John Ford again, and I didn't want to be alone with Ford, because I knew we would get into a fight, and I would beat him up. He was a very unhappy man, and could be nasty.

But Henry and Jack and William Powell were also in that picture, and I like them all. Henry was such a gentle man, and Jack I had recognized as a great talent back in the forties when my brother Bill was running Cagney Productions for me. Bill Powell was so funny. He had a gigantic, protruding rear end, and I did caricatures of all the cast and gave them to each one. All except Powell, who figured that something must be up. So one day when I was napping he slipped into my bungalow and found my drawing of him, with his huge keister, and his knocking knees, and he burst out laughing, which woke me. "Sign it, you S.O.B.!" he laughed. So I signed it for him, and he proudly walked out with my cartoon of him, which I hadn't shown him because I didn't want to hurt his feelings.

Bette Davis

James Cagney was a terrific actor, and there was no one else like him. But I barely remember *Jimmy the Gent*, which we made in 1934. I had practically no part at all in that picture.

Loretta Young

Jimmy Cagney, who in my view was certainly not good looking, never knew that I was wildly in love with him, but I was. I told him years later, when I was on a train taking my son to Purdue. Jimmy, who never flew, was also on the train, and he sent word to us asking if Miss Young and her son would have dinner with him that evening in the private dining car. Well, Peter nearly had a stroke he was so thrilled. Of course that was many, many years after Jimmy and I had made *Taxi* under Roy Del Ruth.

James Cagney

Roy Del Ruth was no director at all. I never knew what he was, other than negative, not some of the time, not most of the time, but all of the time. I did *Blonde Crazy* with Joan Blondell under him in 1931, and then both *Taxi* and *Winner Take All* under him in 1932. Then in 1933 we did *Lady Killer* with Mae Clarke. Despite the limited direction, those four films were well received. I worked with him again much later, in *The West Point Story*, with Doris Day and Virginia Mayo.

Loretta Young

When Jimmy came out here to California to receive his Lifetime Achievement Award, someone kiddingly said to me that I was one he had missed, but I replied that he had not missed me. He hadn't known it, but I was madly in love with him back in the early thirties. I still remember a dream I had about him, during the making of *Taxi*, in which I was in deep water. Well, I can't swim, and never learned how, and in the dream I had fallen into this dirt hole filled with water, where I was drowning. All of my family were standing around the edge saying, "Come on, Gretch,* you can make it! You can climb up the side!" Well, nobody was giving me a hand, and all of a sudden Jimmy Cagney appeared and said, "Hey, this kid needs some help," so he dove in and brought me up, saving me.

Olivia de Havilland

I learned a lot from Jimmy Cagney, and he was always so sweet to me. On *A Midsummer Night's Dream* he was very nice to me, and I was so flattered. He would come into my little canvas dressing room, and we would just talk about everything. I couldn't believe it, for he was already a great star, and it was my first film, way back in 1935.

James Cagney

I played the role of Bottom in *A Midsummer Night's Dream*, alongside Mickey Rooney as Puck. Bottom was set apart from the other roles, and Shakespeare himself depicted Bottom as a ham. Bottom wanted to play all of the parts, so I played him as a ham, with that ass head on my head. The critics didn't seem to like my portrayal, though. That film had a great cast, too,

---

* Loretta Young's Christian name is Gretchen Michaela Young.

with Joe E. Brown, Dick Powell, Arthur Treacher, and many others as well.

Olivia de Havilland

Of course Jimmy and I worked together again, in *The Irish in Us* that same year, and then *The Strawberry Blonde* in 1941. That's where I learned so much from him. Things wouldn't even be in the script, but he would always find things to do to make a scene come alive.

For example, in one scene he had to make an exit, but there was nothing indicated in Julius and Philip Epstein's script to really tie it off. He knew that it was very important for the film that the scene end just right, so he would find some tiny little reaction, like coming around the door again with a comment or a gesture, to keep the interest going. He had a wonderful sense of pace and timing, and he liked me because he said that I listened, which he said lots of actresses did not. I hadn't been aware that that was a special virtue; it seemed a natural thing to do. But what a nice compliment. If you are really inside the character you are bound to listen, I think, especially if the character has decent manners.

James Cagney

On *The Irish in Us* I got to work with Pat O'Brien and Frank McHugh, my two best friends, and Olivia, who was my favorite and most beautiful leading lady.

Olivia de Havilland

Ah, isn't that sweet? I knew he liked working with me, but I never knew I was his favorite. How dear of him!

James Cagney

I recall a scene in *The Irish in Us* where Frank comes back from a formal affair, wearing a full dress suit with a white cap.

Pat looks him over and says, "You didn't wear that cap to the ball, did you?" Frank ad-libbed the reply: "Oh, I know, it should have been black!" Yes, Pat and Frank were my dear friends, and for nearly fifty years Pat was number one, right up until he died. He was kind and funny, and we complimented each other in our performances. When he gave, I took; and when I gave, he took. We had a great working relationship, for he was a fun-loving guy who lived for today and seldom thought about tomorrow. I was fundamentally different from Pat, though, for I enjoy a quiet, less hectic lifestyle. But we sure enjoyed one another's company. He had his stories, too, good old Irish blarney.

That close camaraderie must have shown up on the screen, too, since the studio chose Pat to be my most frequent filmmate—probably because they thought the ladies couldn't stand up to me. I made nine pictures with Pat, and nine with Frank, and among those there were five that the three of us did together.

In one of them, *Boy Meets Girl*, in 1938, we three were teamed with Ralph Bellamy, also a close friend, and Ronald Reagan, whom I liked a great deal. What a nice man, and what a good actor! I remember one night, at a Screen Actors Guild function, when Ronnie made a speech, forty-five minutes long, and all of it was ad-libbed. Well, it was brilliant. I came home to my wife Bill afterward and told her that man was fated, and not as an actor. I was right, too, for he became President, and a great one.

Because Pat, Frank, and I were Irish, and we stuck together, we became known as "The Irish Mafia." We rejected that term, however, and then got to be known as "The Boys' Club." Spencer Tracy was a member of our group, too, and what a talented man he was. He was an actor's actor.

Ava Gardner

One of my biggest regrets was not doing a picture I was offered with Jimmy Cagney. It was one of the worst mistakes I

ever made. I was very busy at the time, being married to Artie
Shaw and running to UCLA to take courses and to get some
kind of education so that I could catch up with my husband,
which was impossible, since he had not only a big head start
on me and a great hunger for knowledge, but since he was also
truly an intellectual.

In retrospect now I realize that I really didn't want to
work, but to play, which is why I failed to make use of the
opportunity to do that film with Cagney. I probably had some
flirt going at the time, and now I don't even know who it was.
They recently had a run of Cagney's old films on television in
London, and my God! He didn't *get* brilliant along the way—
he started off brilliant. He and Bette Davis both started out in
top form. When you see their early work you see it's just as
good now as it was considered to be then, back in the early
thirties, like *The Public Enemy*.

James Cagney

The Public Enemy was the film that really launched my career.
I played a mean, mixed-up hood, a tough kid who tried to
throw his weight around and ended up dead. It was a good
part. I don't think I took anything away from it. It just kind of
flowed along. As you may know, the first title was *Beer and
Blood*. It was one of the first chances I had to portray that kind
of person—the fist-swinging gangster who becomes ruthless
in order to succeed. There were many tough guys to play in
the scripts that Warners kept assigning me. Each of my subse-
quent roles in the hoodlum genre offered the opportunity to
inject something new, which I always tried to do. One could
be funny, and the next one flat. Some roles were mean, and
others were meaner. A few roles among them were actually
sympathetic and kindhearted, and I preferred them, but generally I did not get to do many of those parts until much later
in my career, for the public seemed to prefer me as a bad guy.

Since I was most frequently cast as a criminal, constantly
on the prod, I rarely got to do the comedy roles I really would

have preferred. I am really not at all like the character I played in *The Public Enemy*. I'm chiefly pretty quiet and reserved and private. Nevertheless, I had lots of gangster roles, and too much of the same thing gets to be too much. I don't understand why the public never tired of those awful hoodlums, like in *The Roaring Twenties* and *White Heat*. Originally, Cody Jarrett in *White Heat* was to be portrayed as the standard gangster type. But I decided to give him some flesh, and to develop the role as a homicidal maniac. So, we made him nuts, a psychopath with a mother fixation, occasional fits, and incapacitating headaches. It worked, and the film was a success.

William Wellman did a good job on *The Public Enemy*, I thought, as he did on the earlier picture I did with him, *Other Men's Women*, in which I played opposite Mary Astor and Joan Blondell. He let me go my way and develop my own interpretation whenever it was possible. Having this kind of discernment makes for a good director. With other members of the cast of *The Public Enemy*, especially Jean Harlow, he was less understanding. It was Wellman who suggested that I squash that half a grapefruit into Mae Clarke's face in the famous breakfast scene, and it set a precedent in the abuse of women in films. In my next picture, *Smart Money*, which I made in 1931 with Edward G. Robinson, I again had to hit a lady in the face.

Ava Gardner

I wish to hell I'd done that picture about Ruth Etting with Jimmy Cagney. I think we would have gotten along very well, and it might have changed a lot of people's opinion of my acting ability. But, I turned it down, and so Doris Day starred in it.

James Cagney

I liked Doris Day very much. She was a lovely girl and had a lot of talent. I made *Love Me or Leave Me* with her in 1955, and thought it was a shame that she went the route of *Pillow Talk* after portraying Ruth Etting.

George C. Scott

What a wonderful, kind man Jimmy Cagney has always been. I really love him. I bought some Morgan horses from him when I was married to Pat, my second wife, and I kept them through the third and fourth marriages, both of which were to Colleen Dewhurst, and so now my wife, Trish Van Devere, rides them. She's a brilliant rider.

Lauren Bacall

Bogey always felt that Jimmy Cagney was the greatest personality ever to appear on the screen. I would say that Bogey and Cagney were neck and neck.

James Cagney

Bogey had a real presence as an actor, and he was able to do anything required of him. I made *The Roaring Twenties* with him under Raoul Walsh in 1939. If they were legends then, I didn't know it. They were both just plain people to me. I got along fine with Walsh, for he took suggestions from me for script improvements and incorporated them into the scenes. Actually, I worked with Walsh three more times, too—in *The Strawberry Blonde*, made in 1941 with Olivia de Havilland and Rita Hayworth; in *White Heat*, which came out in 1949; and in *A Lion Is in the Streets*, done in 1953.

Oddly enough, I had already killed Bogey in the other two films I made with him also, *Angels With Dirty Faces* and *The Oklahoma Kid*. I never really got to know the man, however, and for that matter, few people did, for he seemed to have an attitude that nobody was going to like him. The way he dealt with that was to be sure that they knew that he didn't like them first. I'm not at all like that.

Lauren Bacall, ca. 1945

Humphrey Bogart, ca. 1942

Bette Davis

The first time I worked with Bogey was on my very first film, *Bad Sister*, which was produced by Universal back in 1931. We were both under contract to Universal at that point, and somehow both of us ended up in that horrific film. It was the beginning for each of us. He, too, was from the theater, right from the beginning. He played the city slicker, and I played the good sister, and I can't say that I had any idea that he would go on to become one of the top stars of all time.

Conrad Nagel was the hero of *Bad Sister*, and in it there was a scene in which I had to wash a baby. For days and days before I would go to all the crew and ask, "Tell me, is it going to be a boy baby or a girl baby?" Well, my dear, you can imagine what I got! It was a stark-naked baby boy! And there was Mr. Nagel, who played my beau, standing beside me. And on the screen you can see my blush, for in black-and-white film red goes dark gray, and I turned a very dark gray. You can see that my face goes practically black, I was blushing so deeply. I was a very, very Yankee girl, and that kind of thing bothered me a great deal. I was terribly embarrassed to be washing a naked boy with Mr. Nagel right next to me.

There was something else funny that happened on the set of *Bad Sister*, too. One day someone screamed out, "Move that broad to the other side of the room!" Well, I drew myself up to my full height and I said, "Don't you *ever* call me a broad again!" Well, it turned out that "broad" was the name of one of the biggest lights, and they weren't even referring to me. That was one of the funniest things that ever happened to me, getting so upset for no reason at all. I was just a very New England girl, and simply not accustomed to the Hollywood way of talking or doing. It wasn't anything as complicated as feeling defensive. It was that I was insulted, that's all. I thought that I was being called something I didn't believe in. I never went around carrying my sorrows on my sleeve, whether I was doing well or not. Never! I was just furious, though, for back in New England we did not do that, call women "broads."

Lauren Bacall

No star has had the kind of longevity Bogey has had. No other star had such an impact on every generation, and it will go on forever, I expect. I never considered him a leading man, however. He was an actor, and a great personality. He was really a first-rate actor, having been trained on the stage.

Rod Steiger

Bogey had played in seven consecutive hits on Broadway before coming to Hollywood, in one of which he originated the line "Tennis, anyone?" That seems awfully ironic when you consider the gangster parts he later played. Until being cast as the murderer Duke Mantee in *The Petrified Forest* he had always played young society types, and he did come from a very nice family. The stage producer-director Arthur Hopkins heard Bogey's voice and decided that he was the man he wanted to play the part on Broadway. As a result of that he remained almost typecast as a tough. But he was a sweetheart to work with.

Katharine Hepburn

I remember that Arthur Hopkins was considered absolutely insane to cast Bogey as a gangster, but it worked. I think that Bogey was one of the few truly happy people. Of course, Betty Bacall can tell us for sure. He drank out of merriment, and because he liked the taste. The people who had trouble with it drank to escape. He drank too much, but not out of desperation. He was a charming actor, and he won the Oscar for *The African Queen* with me. He had started out playing "mama's boys," for he was very fine and upright and socially a very correct fellow. And then he degenerated into being a killer, while Spencer Tracy started out as a villain and then became a priest.

Lauren Bacall

Bogey thought that Spencer was the best actor of them all. I would rank Bogey, Cagney, and Tracy all at the top, for Bogey was capable of playing many different kinds of roles. He had an incredible personality, a presence. And he was very well brought up. His father was a doctor, and his mother an artist, and he was by no means a kid of the streets. He used to sail boats in the summer, back in the early 1900s. Now that's pretty classy stuff. I didn't know anything about that. I was from the streets of New York, so what did I know about that kind of life? A New York girl like I was just didn't know about such things. Bogey and I had a yacht called the *Santana*, and I loved being on that sailboat, but the sea didn't have the same meaning for me that it did for Bogey. He was in love with the sea. Unless you've had that feeling you cannot possibly understand it.

I remember when *The Old Man and the Sea* came out, and *Time* had a cover story on Hemingway. In that article Hemingway described how he felt about the sea, and I remember Bogey handing me the magazine in bed one night, telling me to read it in order to understand how and why he loved the sea and that boat so much. He felt that it was the last free place on earth, and he was right. When I was out on the *Santana* with him I adored it, but I resented the fact that since we had this expensive boat we had to take it out every weekend. We never had a choice, and I didn't like the sense of obligation. It was like a house I had in the country. It was expensive to keep it, and that got to be a bore, since it became a duty, rather than a pleasure. I didn't want to *have* to use it, but I had to, because in each case it was there.

Ava Gardner

I made *The Barefoot Contessa* with Bogey in 1954, and frankly he wasn't one of my favorite people to work with. He was a nice enough guy, I guess, but I never really knew him. For me he was not like Clark Gable and Robert Taylor and Greg Peck and the others. Maybe Katie Hepburn saw a different side of him, and knew him better than I did, because when you're down in Africa working together, and especially with that wonderful John Huston along, it's bound to bring you together. Bogey and I just did our scenes together, and that was it.

Rossano Brazzi

I thought that Humphrey Bogart was an actor who could work magic. Underneath that tough, cynical exterior there was such tenderness, such goodness. I will never forget the night we finished shooting *The Barefoot Contessa*. We had dinner in Rome, and on the back of my license he wrote down his home address and telephone number. "Now I want you to let me know when you're coming to America," he said, "so that I can plan something special for you." One week after I got back to Hollywood he had one hundred people over at his house for a beautiful party in my honor.

Lauren Bacall

I had seen Bogey on film in *Casablanca* in New York before going out to Hollywood to make *To Have and Have Not* in 1944, as well as in anything he had made with Bette Davis, such as *The Petrified Forest*. Actually, I was in love with Leslie Howard as a kid. He was my dream man, and my idea of heaven. So, my preconception of Humphrey Bogart was that he was a good actor, but not my type, not at all. I had no stars in my eyes about him. I wasn't attracted to him for an eighth of a second. You see how curious life can be. But who knows how a romance develops? There is a chemistry that happens between two people, and you cannot possibly explain it.

What happened between Bogey and me was certainly not by design. I mean I had been introduced to him before we started filming, but just to say, "How do you do?" First of all, I would never have anything to do with a married man. It would just never occur to me. But we were there together, and we had fun together, and our personalities kind of clicked. The next thing we knew we were getting caught up in something. I mean it didn't happen the first minute, and it was hard for him, too, for he was not a playboy. He didn't fool around, and until he met me he was faithful to Mayo, who was his third wife. He was not a man who screwed around, and to do it when he was married to someone else was a horror to him. He just didn't believe in that kind of thing. She might have been a little ill mentally toward the end, a bit paranoid, but she was definitely an alcoholic. Actually, she was a good actress, a supporting player who had done good work on the stage, but was drunk all the time. She was also very jealous, terribly possessive of Bogey, and it was not a happy situation for him. But, he had more or less accepted that that was how life was going to be, and he wasn't looking for anything else.

He couldn't believe that this new love affair was really happening to him, that he could feel this way about someone else. He probably never believed for a minute that it could work, either. He was twenty-five years my senior, and I was so young. He told me later that he figured I would leave him in five years, because I didn't know anything about life and the world at that point. He fully expected me to take off with someone else one day. But he was a lot more entertaining than anyone else I had ever met, I can tell you. I know that Bogey told Peter Lorre his feelings, and Lorre said, "Well, five years is better than nothing." I think that contributed to Bogey's decision to divorce Mayo and marry me. She was his third wife, and three failed marriages can make you pretty pessimistic. Each of his wives had been an actress, too, but there had not been any children. He was not about to risk it all again, for he had become gun shy. I suppose that every marriage has its problems, and you can never know exactly what goes on behind closed doors between two people. But then after all most movie people are pretty attractive physically, and you're thrown together to make films on location very often, so who knows? You begin to live your part, I guess. Some people must believe it's the real thing when it isn't, and I think that's the main problem. They think they're in love, but they're not, and then it just doesn't work out.

Bogey was very firm about coming home at six o'clock, when you left the acting behind and returned to reality. That was part of his professional theater training, I'd say. Moviemaking is a different thing altogether, for it often finds you working far away from home for a long time. I never went on location to shoot a film. Part of the agreement before we got married was that I would not take off and leave him behind. He said to me, "If you want to follow your career, God bless you; go ahead and do it. But you can't do that and be married at the same time." That was a lesson he had learned from his first three marriages.

So, when he went on location, I went with him, to Africa to make *The African Queen*, and to Mexico to make *The Treasure of the Sierra Madre*, or wherever it was. He was right about that, too, for he knew that marriages don't thrive on separation. There just is too much temptation. Actors are emotional and insecure beings. Being married to an actor is not the ideal state for anyone, as I well know, having married two of them. But I always did believe in putting my marriage first, and I'm not sorry I did. I got very perturbed about my career not doing very well, but I'm glad I made the choice I did.

Robert Stack

I knew Bogey a long time ago, going back to 1950. We were going to do a movie in England called *The Gift Horse*, and we ran into problems because the British were demanding that English actors play English roles. It was the old Equity problem. Anyway, we got over there, and there happened to be an actor who put in a protest, perhaps rightly so. Well, at about ten one evening I got a call from Bogey, who said, "Kid, they're not gonna give you the work permit, and someone's gonna call you tomorrow to inform you. Now this is what you're gonna tell him: that you don't know why you didn't get the work permit, but you understand that this is a union that protects actors, that is supposed to represent their interests. You tell him that you, believing that the union is acting in your interest, but not understanding why this was done, nonetheless have to agree with their decision."

Well, I did what he said, and the next day there were headlines in the papers about the union doing this terrible thing to Robert Stack, a good union man, who never understood the reason. They said that I was in a suite at the Dorchester Hotel, wondering where my next job was coming from. That was very big of Bogey, to take the time to find out what was going on and then to tell me what to say, and to arrange for this media coverage. He obviously had an intelligence connection into Equity, and he used it to help me. I was very lucky to have had Gable, Tracy, and Bogey to guide me.

Bette Davis

The first film I made after I lost my court case against Warners and came back to Hollywood from London was *Marked Woman*, in 1937. That was really a very interesting film, with Bogey and some of the others, including Mayo Methot, his third wife. That was also the beginning of Mr. Thomas Dewey, the state's attorney, who was nominated for President. *Marked Woman* was his story, of how he finally put an end to those gangsters. It was also the first script by Bob Rossen, who later became one of the great screenwriters and directors. Jack Warner had all the great young screenwriters back then. That's how the studio turned out so many wonderful topical films.

Audrey Hepburn

I made *Sabrina* in 1954 with Humphrey Bogart and William Holden under Billy Wilder, and each of them was very kind and gentle and patient with me. One of the most deeply felt senses of gratitude I hold is that, while working in the company of the best actors and best directors, one simply can't miss. It's like playing tennis with a real champ, and as a result of it your game improves. Each of them sent me the ball in such a way that I couldn't miss returning it, with a minimum of good instinct or experience. Of course, I heard about the fights among the three of them, but I was completely oblivious to all that. I was literally thrilled to be working with them, so whatever went on among them—and all of them were very strong characters—I cannot say. I was so green at that stage of my career that I was totally unaware of any such things.

In the case of *Sabrina*, Billy Wilder really wanted to cast me in it, for he had seen *Roman Holiday*, which I had made the year before with Gregory Peck under Willie Wyler. I was under contract to Paramount at the time, where Billy was working, too. But unlike *Roman Holiday*, *Sabrina* was shot entirely in America, in Hollywood and on Long Island. Bill and Bogey played wealthy brothers in it, and I became good friends with Bill during the making of it. In fact, we did another movie together years later, *Paris When It Sizzles*. That movie wasn't around for very long, but it was fun to make, and by that time Bill and I had become great friends.

Bogey was married to Lauren Bacall when we made *Sabrina*, and I just adored her. I used to go to their house. She was divine, so glamorous and nice. I found Betty to be a very warm person. Actually, it was during the making of *Sabrina* that I began one of my very closest and most enduring friendships, with the great designer Hubert de Givenchy. It may be the closest and dearest friendship of them all for me.

Sabrina is the story of a girl whose father is the chauffeur for a very wealthy family. She is sent to Paris, where there is a metamorphosis, and she comes back looking very Parisian, so the son and heir to the family fortune falls in love with her. Well, I asked Edith Head about this, and by the way Edith is another saint. I suggested to her that it might be a good idea for me to pick up the clothes in Paris for the film. Edith had no ego, and was very generous, even though she was head of costumes for Paramount. Someone else might have said, "Oh, no! It would be much better if the clothes were designed by me right here at Paramount." Instead, she agreed, and thought it would be a great idea for me to go to Paris and to find the clothes I liked.

Well, shortly after that I found myself in Paris, and a lady from Paramount's Paris office was helping me, but it was a very bad time of the season, if you know what I mean, for all the couturiers were getting their collections ready for presentation. The designers are more or less shut down at that time of year, and the clientele as a rule does not go to shop when the new collections are being readied for showing to the buyers and the media. In fact, the shows were just two days off.

Well, she took me to Balenciaga, and it was all shut down, so she said to me, "Since we've been to the most established, the dean of the designers, and there is nothing to be seen, why don't we pay a visit to the youngest and the newest? Maybe he will have something for you." I agreed, and so we headed over to Givenchy, who was still young and just starting out, with a small outfit. I tried on everything that was available, and Hubert came downstairs from his workroom to meet with us, and soon I had picked up the famous black-and-white dress, as well as the suit I wore when I was picked up at the station in *Sabrina*. Actually, I've had so many letters from young girls, wanting to know where they could get that dress, hoping that they could be married in it. It was only after making my third film for Paramount, *War and Peace*, that I was able to return to Givenchy and buy his dresses for myself. He is not only a brilliant, gifted designer, but also my dear, close friend. And as you know, I ended up marrying Bogey at the end of *Sabrina*.

Rod Steiger

I did a picture with Bogey called *The Harder They Fall*, which I think was pretty good. It was a boxing story based loosely on the career of Primo Carnera. I played a ruthless fight promoter, and Humphrey Bogart played a reporter in it. It was his last picture, and he died about two months after we completed it. Bogey was one of the nicest men I ever met, too. He had a great sense of humor, and enormous discipline. If an extra had a line, he would stand off-camera and deliver his line, even if it were just "No." Mr. Bogart was just wonderful to work with.

Lauren Bacall

I don't think you ever fully recover from the loss of someone who is very important to your life. But you live with it as well as you can. As I've said, I don't live in the past, and I don't spend my time mulling over what was, or what might have been. It's been so long, though, that I no longer think of Bogey as "my husband."

I would say that as an actor his best work was in *The Treasure of the Sierra Madre* and *The Caine Mutiny* and *The African Queen*. For my money he was the definitive detective, as Sam Spade in *The Maltese Falcon* and as Philip Marlowe in *The Big Sleep*. I don't think that what he did in *Casablanca* was all that great. *Beat the Devil* has become a cult movie, but I haven't seen it in a long time. It was the only time I wasn't with Bogey on location. I was making *How to Marry a Millionaire* at the same time, so I met him in London after it was over. That was the only time we were separated. I think that *Beat the Devil* will last because it had a wonderful cast, as well as a fabulous script.

Anyway, Bogey died in 1957, and I sold the house and moved away in 1959. I had no life in Hollywood any longer. Having once had a great life in that house, I found that I just had nothing to keep me there. I hadn't been thought of as an actress for many years by that point. I was thought of simply as Bogey's wife. My career was less than startling, shall we say.

Geraldine Fitzgerald

I thought that Bogey was lots of fun, and he was the first one to point out to me that my attitude was quite incorrect. He told me that all I had to do was to say "Yes," and that the rest would take care of itself. I guess that I was saying "No" from my experience at the Abbey Theatre in Dublin and with the Mercury Theatre in New York with Orson Welles and John Houseman. Bogey told me that I must simply say "Yes" when I was offered a part in a picture, and for decades after that I would say to myself that I was going to do what Bogey had told me, to say "Yes" to everything that came my way. But I never did. I thought that one had to choose very carefully and make sure that all of the artistic elements of the production were right. What rubbish! By being so choosy you don't have such a good time, for one thing. The original impulse of all the great theatrical people was to do everything, and that is why everyone had such a lovely time. I finally realized that if I said "Yes" more often I would have more lovely times. Bogey's point was that you could never control the end result of a project. That was simply beyond the power of an actor, so you might just as well do everything.

Then one day the time came when I found myself having lunch with Bogey and Ingrid Bergman on the Warner lot, during the filming of *Casablanca*. They both were asking me to help find a way to get out of this terrible film they were in. "This is the worst script we have ever come across," Bogey said to me. "It's true," Ingrid said. "We can't believe the lines. It's just a fright!" I remember how upset Ingrid was. "You know," she said, "I am spoken of as the most beautiful woman in Europe, and that's silly. Everyone knows that I look like a milkmaid, and it embarrasses me. Everyone will laugh at me, and I just don't want to be in a picture like this!"

I saw it again last night on television, and everything about it is sublime. *Casablanca* is a masterpiece, and it just goes to show you that the actors have no control over the final product. Both Bogey and Ingrid were absolutely perfect in it, too.

Ingrid Bergman, ca. 1939

The only reason that they didn't get out of completing it was that both of them would have been sued by Warner and enjoined from making anything else for quite a while. They had both been given enough of a tender to make *Casablanca* that there was no way to get out of it. It was as if they both went in chains to the set every day to make this travesty of a picture that they hated. Bogey proved his own point to me in that picture, and when I saw *Casablanca* I began to take what he had said very seriously. *Casablanca* had started out without even a script and it turned out to be a masterpiece.

Joan Fontaine

Ingrid Bergman was the first actress who didn't pretend to be a glamour queen. She acted like the girl next door, and took off her makeup and high heels, stripping herself of all glamour, and as a result had twice as much glamour as anyone else. She had so much style.

Helen Hayes

I made *Anastasia* with Ingrid Bergman in 1956, and she won the Oscar for it. She was really a star. I had known her since 1940, when she was doing *Liliom* on Broadway with Burgess Meredith. She came out to Nyack to see Charlie and me, and Burgess also had a place up the Hudson, back when he was married to Paulette Goddard. Ingrid would come over and play tennis with Charlie. I got to know her quite well, and I liked her a great deal. She had the most beautiful features, and was always a great dear. What a shame that she is gone, too.

Lauren Bacall

I made *Murder on the Orient Express* with Ingrid Bergman in 1974, and she won an Oscar for that, too. I really think that that had the greatest all-star cast ever, with John Gielgud, Wendy Hiller, Richard Widmark, Sean Connery, Albert Finney, Rachel Roberts, Vanessa Redgrave, and a number of others, too. Ingrid was a lovely woman, but so sad. I had known her a little before we made the film, and we got along well together. We liked one another. She had bigger bones than I, but was not too tall by today's standards. I mean we're all shrimps these days. They're all giants today. Ingrid was very friendly, but not gushy. She was reserved. She loved to work, too, just adored it, and she was very professional. She might have been ill during the making of that picture, but none of us knew it if she was, since she didn't behave as if she was. I don't know if she had had surgery by then, or knew she was going to have it, or what.

Rossano Brazzi

I remember when Roberto Rossellini called me from the airport when he arrived in Hollywood in order to take Ingrid Bergman away. He asked me to come get him at eleven-thirty at night, since he had only three dollars. I picked him up at one o'clock in the morning, brought him back to my house, called Ingrid Bergman, and got them together. She had apparently sent a letter to him saying, probably in innocence and out of respect for his work, "I love you." Well, for the Italians such a thing means that you are in love. The next day I took Roberto, Ingrid, and director Jean Negulesco to lunch at the Beverly Hills Hotel. Jean was a true man of the world, but I had to translate for both Roberto and Ingrid, since she spoke no Italian, and he no English. At the end of the lunch Jean turned to me and said, "Rossano, you won't have to translate for these two any longer, because tomorrow morning they will be in bed together."

I gave Roberto the money to make the first documentary ever filmed in Italy. I was actually making *Vulcano* with Anna Magnani over there when Roberto was shooting *Stromboli* with Ingrid. I took Roberto to see Darryl Zanuck to talk about making that picture. We had an appointment at eleven-thirty, but when we got there I found that Roberto didn't have the script with him. "It is in my mind," he said. Well, things were not done like that back then. I remember that I had to translate his ideas to Zanuck while we were sitting there.

In the old RKO Studio on Washington Boulevard I finally talked Howard Hughes into making the picture. Hughes was the only one who would agree to make *Stromboli*, because he was the only producer who was at all like Rossellini—kind of eccentric and sensitive, I suppose. He didn't care about the script, but he was enchanted by Roberto, and he liked Ingrid. So, Roberto left America with Ingrid, and while they were in Italy I got a call to come to Italy also, to shoot *Vulcano* with Anna Magnani, to be directed by William Dieterle.

Every night after we finished shooting Anna would walk to the edge of the island of Vulcano, off the coast of Sicily, and look over to the little island of Stromboli, where Roberto was filming *Stromboli* with Ingrid. There were three hundred of us living in tents, but Anna would march to the beach and shout "You son of a bitch!" You see, Anna and Roberto had lived together for seven years before this, and he had suddenly walked out on her to take up with Ingrid. She couldn't stand it. I remember the day Anna died in Rome, in 1973. They called me from the clinic to tell me that Anna wanted to see me. I went down and she whispered to me, "Roberto? Roberto?" Rossellini had taken a plane to America to get a cancer specialist, for she had it in her spine. The next day she died, and that afternoon Roberto landed with the doctor. Roberto was very much in love with Anna, but he had many women. He had a lot of charm, and was always a ladies' man.

Gregory Peck

I think you fall in love a little bit with a woman like Ingrid Bergman, and I don't think there's any way to avoid it, for she was incredibly beautiful, and a very sweet person. She was maybe twenty-seven or twenty-eight at the time Hitchcock shot *Spellbound* with the two of us, and I was about the same age, and why would I want to avoid falling in love with

Ingrid? Her lovely skin kind of took your breath away, and her whole radiance was something to behold. She was in full flower back then, and extremely ambitious to do fine work, to do her best.

I think that eventually led her down the garden path to Roberto Rossellini, because she didn't do good work with him. She was so impressed with those neorealist films that he made that she forgot who she was. She wanted so to be an artist that she embraced this neorealism of Rossellini's and Vittorio De Sica's and only too late realized that they, too, could make potboilers. She bought what Rossellini was selling lock, stock, and barrel, which is a shame.

It was understandable to a lot of people who knew her that she could fly the coop of Hollywood, for she thought about going back to the theater to make use of her talent and whatever else she had. Actually, I think that Rossellini was something of a predator, and for all her ambition she was still pretty innocent. It ultimately cost her a great deal, for he was here in Hollywood only about a day and a half, and the next thing you knew she had flown off to Italy with him to make some crazy thing called *Stromboli*.

None of the films she made with him ever came off, and eventually she grew disillusioned and moved out. He was extremely talented, but at the same time basically a spoiled Italian fat boy, one who wanted everything he wanted right when he wanted it. In the long run he wasn't fit for her, and it's just too bad that she had to run off at all. But if she did, what a pity it wasn't Louis Malle, or François Truffaut, or Michelangelo Antonioni, or Federico Fellini.

Gina Lollobrigida

Federico Fellini asked me to do *La Dolce Vita*, the role that Anouk Aimée played. But my ex-husband, who was managing my career at that time, never told me. It was a great disappointment for me when I discovered what had happened. You know, you can't judge a Fellini script, because it is all in his mind. Probably the script did not seem good enough, so my ex-husband declined it for me without even telling me that it had been offered to me. For many years Fellini was angry with me, and when I found out that my ex-husband had refused it I didn't have the guts to tell Fellini that it had not been my decision. I recently told Fellini that I would play an extra for him at any time. We shall see.

Marcello Mastroianni

Something happened for me after *La Dolce Vita* came out, for in America it was a successful film. I think that it was through this film that people began to think of me as a sexy Latin lover. The publicity people and journalists who wrote about it thought it would be good to portray me that way. This one is a gangster, and this one is a cowboy, and this one is a lover.

But I really can't understand what this type means. Perhaps what I think it means is very different from what the American public thinks a sexy Latin lover is. Is it romantic? And at my age? I am nearly seventy years old. But I would like to have three or four years left! Fifty years old is a very nice age, I think. When I am asked about this image I say, "But you have never seen my films. If you had seen the old ones, you would never have found a character so 'amateur' and 'macho.' " I have made a number of films with Federico Fellini, and the leading character in all of them is his own image: an intellectual, an artist who is lost in a complicated life. He is always somebody fragile, never a macho.

In *La Dolce Vita*, for example, I played a naive, provincial journalist trying to get a story. I am used by a woman, Anouk Aimée, who tells me that she wants to make love to me while she is kissing another man. So, where is the conquistador? In *8½* I played another very fine character, but sensitive. He is caught in the classic Italian triangle: wife, mistress, and himself. He is completely impotent in the situation—not sexually, but he is an intellectual, not a macho. Then I made *Casanova '70*, and more impotence. He can't make love unless he is in danger. He needs it to be excited.

Marcello Mastroianni, ca. 1960

A beautiful film I made was *Il Bell'Antonio*, about a young, impotent Sicilian man, and it was pretty successful in America. Yes, this handsome Anthony is married to Claudia Cardinale, when she was young and beautiful, but he can't make love; he is completely impotent. And in Sicily, this is terrible, for it is a question of honor. What a situation! And then I made *A Special Day* with Sophia Loren, and I played a homosexual in that one. I even played a man who got pregnant, in *The Most Important Event Since Man Walked on the Moon*, a French film with Catherine Deneuve. So, if I am pregnant, homosexual, and impotent, how can I be a sexy Latin lover?

But Sophia is my favorite actress, and indeed my favorite colleague. I love her very much. We grew up together in the cinema. We have made ten films together, which might be a record, and we are really very good friends. She is an intelligent woman, and a Neopolitan, so she has a sense of humor, too. We like each other very much. I like to work with people who are both beautiful and nice. Sophia has it all, like Anna Magnani did: beauty, brains, intelligence, elegance.

Rossano Brazzi

Anna Magnani was not beautiful, but it is true that she was the best of the Italian actresses. She was like the Italian Bette Davis: very talented, but not pretty. For me, these kinds of faces are more important than the beautiful ones. They have more character for the cinematographic form.

I had a close friend who was one of them, and we used to go to Santa Monica to have a cup of coffee with the simple fishermen. That was Spencer Tracy. He was a very good actor, for everything that he was thinking or feeling came out in his face. He didn't need to say a word to communicate exactly what he was supposed to. And yet he was not a handsome man. But what a face! I met him also back in 1948, when I met everyone.

I remember that as soon as I arrived in Hollywood I went

to see Alida Valli, who had already moved to America from
Italy. At that time she was at RKO, and she had just finished
The Paradine Case with Gregory Peck under Alfred Hitchcock. I remember that she was just about to start another
picture, and she introduced me to a gentleman who was with
her, saying, "This is Cary Grant." He asked me if I had a car,
which I did not, and so he offered to drive me home. That was
the kind of solidarity that operated in Hollywood back then.

Audrey Hepburn

Every time that I see Sophia Loren I feel that I know her well,
but our paths do not cross as frequently as you might expect.
She has this marvelous inner quality, a profoundly truthful
nature that seems to radiate from her very being. I like her a
lot.

Gregory Peck

I love Sophia, for she's so full of life, so full of fun. Again, it's
hard not to be in love with Sophia Loren, and who wouldn't
want to be? She has the most wonderful musical laugh. Marcello once said that Sophia is the kind of woman you want to
settle down with and have some kids. I believe he was right
about that. That's what Carlo Ponti did, and it worked out
somewhat better than the affair between Ingrid and Roberto.
   She's a very natural actress, with a kind of beauty and
appeal like no one else. She is just all woman. I love her still,
and we had great fun making *Arabesque*, back in 1966. I
always have fun when we go to see her, which is not that
often. I wish that someone would come up with something for
her to do, for she loves to work, and she's ready to work now,
I think. She has had a problem getting good scripts, though.
We had a running gin game going during the making of
Arabesque, and even though the games were for small stakes I
think I ended up paying her $1,400. We would grab ten or
twenty minutes here and there, and she would keep score.

Maybe that was the Neapolitan way of doing it; she had a strange rule about wrapping a run around the corner, going from king to ace to deuce. She had quite a few variations like that.

I recall having to rescue her in a scene in a wheat field with a grain harvester bearing down on us. The villain and his toughies were trying to run us down and thresh us, so Sophia and I were running away. The script said that I was pulling her, but since she could run faster than I she was getting ahead of me, so I would have to pull her back. Finally I said to Stanley Donen, the director of *Arabesque*, "Look, Stanley, I'm supposed to be rescuing Sophia, but she's rescuing me!" Sophia then said that I should run faster, and I said, "Goddammit, I can't, and you know it!" It was my bum ankle again. But she's just great fun to be with, and enjoys the day's work so much. I do wish that somebody would come up with a good script for Sophia. She could perform like Eleanora Duse with the right script, and you know she won the Oscar the first time she was nominated, for that Italian picture called *Two Women*. It was back in 1960, and the only time she was nominated.

Rossano Brazzi

I made *Timbuktu* with Sophia and John Wayne back in 1958 way out in the Sahara Desert, and I watched it on television three weeks ago. I happened to see Sophia a few days ago at one of the film festivals, but I have really lost track of her, for she lives in Geneva, Paris, and New York most of the time.

Loretta Young

I made a couple of pictures with John Wayne back in the early thirties, and I knew him well. In fact, Duke and Josie were married in my house. Josephine was my sister's best friend, so of course we saw a lot of Duke. They went together seven years before they were married.

One night at a party after *The Cowboys*, in the early seventies, Duke asked me to dance, and I remember that he said, "Gee, Gretch, would you believe this now?" I said, "No, not in a thousand years," for there was a time when Spencer Tracy kidded Duke—he would say, "I don't know how you get a job, because you can't act your way out of a paper bag!" "I know it," Duke replied, "but I'm there ahead of you, kid!" The two of them used to fight like a couple of kids that way. They were really very cute together.

I don't know, but I think it was just Duke's charisma and his niceness that got him so many parts. I mean he made over two hundred fifty films. He was an innately nice man. His oldest child, Michael, is my godson. Duke really was a "good guy," and it showed. He was attractive, and he was reasonable, and there was nothing vain about him, even when he was young and handsome. He never thought so, though. But when he got old and ugly he still wasn't ugly, because he was so nice to everyone.

Robert Stack

I made a good picture with Duke Wayne in 1954 called *The High and the Mighty*. It was about an airliner in trouble over the Pacific, and William Wellman directed it. Wellman scared the hell out of me. He got performances out of people by terrorizing them. I remember Doe Avedon, who played the stewardess, and in one scene she was walking up the aisle when Wellman shouted out, "What's the matter with you, Avedon? Can't you even walk straight?" She replied, "Mr. Wellman, you've got me so frightened my knees won't work!"

He was of the old school, a big fat hero who liked Jack Pershing, and he had a steel plate in his head from a war wound. He was a member of the Lafayette Escadrille, too, a corps for Americans who had volunteered to fight for France. Wellman was far from stupid, and really no more bizarre than anyone else. He was very adept at getting actors emotionally aroused, and he did it any way he saw fit, usually by keeping the pressure on them. The camera picks up what you are

John Wayne, ca. 1948

feeling, so however he went about making you feel what he wanted was okay, since it worked.

Underneath his gruff exterior, though, Bill Wellman was a sweetheart, and very soft. In fact, I owe him a great deal, because Duke Wayne had promised the part I got to Bob Cummings, and it was over Duke's objections that Wellman believed in me enough to give me this part that everyone in town wanted, in a picture that Duke himself was producing.

James Stewart

In person Duke Wayne was just like Duke Wayne in the movies, and in my view Duke and Henry Fonda were the very best actors of them all. Duke was a very strong, fine man, full of determination and high ideals. He was dead set on what he believed, and he was never embarrassed to say what he thought, or to show how he felt. He was a quiet man, and perhaps the quietest man I ever knew.

He and John Ford were very dear friends for many years, and in fact like a father and son. On the other hand, when they were making a picture Ford would never let Duke off the hook. He was on his back the whole time. He would let Duke get through an entire scene, and then yell "Cut!" before turning to Duke and say, "That scene was fine, but Duke, why on earth did you make that strange move? You embarrass all of us when you do those things!" Oh, I mean Ford was so hard on Duke you would just cringe. But that's just the way Ford operated.

I'll never forget when the three of us were making *The Man Who Shot Liberty Valance* back in 1962 how Ford would get on Duke, and Duke would just stand there and take it for as long as he could. Then finally they would both just walk away. Well, one day Duke came up to me and said, "Hey, Jim, how is it that you get away without any of this? Why does he always have to do it to me? Why doesn't he let you have any of this?"

Three or four days later I was talking to Woody Strode, a

wonderful black actor who was in the film, and for some reason Ford called me over to ask what I thought of the costume Woody was wearing. Now why on earth I said this I don't know, but I said, "Well, it looks a little Uncle Remus-y, doesn't it?" Ford just looked at me, and then he said to the assistant director, "Would you blow the whistle? Twice." Then he turned back to me and said, "Would you come with me, please?"

I walked with Ford out into the middle of the set with all the lights on, and he called up to see if everyone could hear him, then asked everyone to gather around. "I just want to announce that we have a racist in our company, a man who has a low regard for the black man," he announced. "I didn't want to let this go by without letting all of you know this disgrace that is in our midst. If any future trouble erupts about race, this man is probably behind it. Now get back to work." Then he dismissed me and sent me to my dressing room while everyone else returned to work. I was silently walking back to my dressing room, so humiliated I couldn't even speak, and then I felt a tap on my back. I turned around to find Duke there, and he was just beaming. "That's fine now," he said to me. It was all a part of the game of making movies with John Ford.

SCENE SIX

Tossed Salad

A S THE CLOCK STRIKES NINE the waiters refill the golden chalices of the twenty-four guests with aged wine from the San Simeon cellar. After the dinner plates are removed a mammoth salad is placed in front of each of them, who by now are growing very accustomed to the fabulous surroundings in this remote castle high above the sea. It is apparent that their host is not going to join them for dinner, but they seem not to mind, as a serenade from a string quartet wafts from some unseen room into the stately Refectory.

Continuing the portrait of Duke Wayne, Jimmy Stewart again raises the memory of director John Ford, under whom they both worked. Evidently, one good director calls to mind another, for the train of thought quickly moves on to Howard Hawks, and then to John Huston, whose direction of Katharine Hepburn in *The African Queen* and Gregory Peck in *Moby Dick* provides more colorful anecdotes.

Billy Wilder and Frank Capra also receive evaluations as directors, and the strange tale of *It's a Wonderful Life* is revealed by Stewart, who then turns to Jean Harlow, who gave the young actor his first real kiss. A discussion of the platinum actress ensues, leading the guests to assess the unique popularity of Stewart himself. Then George C. Scott draws the parallel between Stewart and Gary Cooper as quintessential Hollywood Royals. Even reticent Rod Steiger describes Coop as a "sweetheart," which prompts some of Cooper's many leading ladies, including Audrey Hepburn,

Lauren Bacall, Geraldine Fitzgerald, and Loretta Young, to recall his sensitivity.

The course concludes with a collective character portrait of this favorite leading man, just as the butler announces that dessert will be served around the incredible indoor pool, which is in another building altogether. The two dozen stars slowly rise and begin to escort each other through yet another grand portal into a labyrinth of intimate chambers, where the coffered medieval ceilings and superb treasures invite examination.

James Stewart

John Ford was the director I found to be the most explicit about how film should be first and foremost a visual medium. He was, of course, a man who had a lot to say about a lot of things, but about this subject he was very definite. "If you can't tell your story up there on the screen without resorting to the spoken word," I remember his saying, "then you're not using the motion picture medium correctly." I firmly believe that he was entirely right in this assessment.

When we were making *Liberty Valance* with Duke, and I thought things were going along just fine, suddenly Ford would shout, "Cut!" We would stop and look at each other, wondering what we had done wrong, and then Ford would say, "Everybody's talking too much! Now I don't have that line of yours in my script," he said, pointing at me, "and I don't know where you got all of that stuff you've been saying," he said to Duke. Now this was not true, because Ford knew every word of everyone's part, and he sensed that there was too much talking going on. So, he would call a conference and sit us down around a table to go over the script. I've seen him cut at least a quarter of the script. He would whittle the words down to the bare bones, and it would work much better, especially in a western setting. Ford just didn't like too much dialogue.

Lauren Bacall

I wish that I had worked under John Ford, too. Bogey knew him well, since they had worked together in the early days. Ford had a boat, too, so I met him on Catalina. He was on his boat, and we were on ours. He was a great old character, and a marvelous director.

Howard Hawks had a very distinguished career, too, directing all kinds of pictures, comedies and westerns and thrillers and romances. He was very intimidating when I first met him. I was terrified of him, and he scared me to death. I had never met anyone like Howard, and still haven't. But he sure knew how to use the camera, and he always had great byplay between the men and the women in his stories. He always liked women who behaved like men, too. He thought that was sexy. He was an odd man. Finally I became very fond of him, for he taught me a lot. His movies will last a long time, as long as film lasts.

I love *The Big Sleep*, which I made with Bogey and Hawks in 1946. People like to say that the plot of it makes no sense, but it didn't matter then and it doesn't matter now, because it's a *great* movie. It had a wonderful cast, and the characters were fabulous, and it was in black and white, which is my favorite. I think this Colorization is inexcusable. They ruined *The Maltese Falcon* when they painted it pink and green. It's shocking, and all a matter of greed, and it will backfire on them. I don't think they've colorized *The Big Sleep* yet, or *To Have and Have Not*.

I was still quite innocent underneath the veneer of sultry wisdom when we made that one, in 1944. I suppose that that is one of the reasons it worked so well. I believe that my underlying innocence, in combination with the suggestive dialogue and the attitude I struck, made it better than it would have been had I been a woman of the world. I didn't know *anything* back then, including what I was doing. Everything I did in *To Have and Have Not* was pure instinct. I was only nineteen years old, and far from an experienced actress. I was so nervous that I had to hold my chin down to keep my head from shaking. That's what they called "The Look." It's really the most ridiculous way some things happen. It looked like a hot come-on, and it worked. Hawks really knew what to do, and he's the one who should be given credit for that. He was a great moviemaker. My character was named for his wife, Slim, who had discovered me in *Harper's Bazaar*, where I was a model.

James Cagney

Howard Hawks was a gentleman, and I liked him a great deal, for he allowed the actors to play the roles as themselves. *The Crowd Roars*, which I made with him in 1932, was an inspired film, in scope at least, because of Howard's use of sudden camera cuts. He made deliberate efforts to authenticate through dramatic activity the themes of that picture. It was very original for 1932. In *Ceiling Zero*, which we made in 1935, we moved the same kind of fast action and suspense from the race car track to the air, with terrifying results. I crashed in the final scene.

Douglas Fairbanks, Jr.

Howard Hawks was very tough in a silent way. He was very quiet and firm, so very few people took liberties with him. He was just icy cold, and austere, just as unemotional as anyone I have ever known. But he knew what other people's emotions were, and he knew how to get them onto the screen, which is where it counted.

He was stiff and correct and highly methodical when we made *The Dawn Patrol* in 1930. Richard Barthelmess was the star of that one, and I was simply the top featured player, with Neil Hamilton. It was later remade with Errol Flynn and David Niven, and in the later version they used the filmed sequences of the airborne parts from the one I was in, recutting it to make it seem different. All of the air battles and crashes were taken from the original, which Howard had directed. All the studios did that if they could, using footage from one film twenty years later in a completely different film, in order to save money. That was common practice for navy battles and westerns, with stampedes and wild chases.

But Howard was always very definite and proper, and there was very little about him that was impulsive.

Lauren Bacall

Of all those brilliant directors, though, I think John Huston was the best. He was a genius, and he directed *Key Largo*. My first encounter with Huston had been much before that, though, since he and Bogey had been friends for many years. They were very close, ever since making *The Maltese Falcon*, which was John's directing debut. I knew him socially, and then went on location to Mexico with them for *The Treasure of the Sierra Madre* in 1948. He was great to actors, so working with him was a wonderful experience.

Katharine Hepburn

I think that John Huston was a brilliant romantic. In his autobiography John told a story incorrectly about a wonderful piece of direction he gave me when we were making *The African Queen*. The first thing we shot was Robert Morley's funeral, and I had a big hat on, but the climate in the Congo was so damp that the brim sagged and wilted. I remember how we used to make a stiffener out of boiled rice juice to keep it firm. It was sopping wet, and there I was, kneeling in the mud, with no wardrobe woman. I guess *I* was the wardrobe woman.

Anyway, Doris Langley Moore, who designed the costumes, was the daughter of a missionary, and she said, "You've got to get materials where you can just scrape off the dirt, and where they can't tell if you're soaking wet from sweat or from humidity." Solving those problems was rather fun.

Katharine Hepburn, ca. 1940

Well, John saw the first day's work, and he came over to me and said, "I don't know what to say to you, but did you ever see a newsreel of Eleanor Roosevelt going to visit the people in the hospital?" I had, as it happened. So he said, "Now Mrs. Roosevelt was not a beautiful woman, so she smiled, the way a minister's sister would smile. When you're not smiling you mouth goes down, and your cheeks get hollow, and your eyes are not as bright. But when you smile, anything is excusable." Well, it was a brilliant piece of direction. That was all he said to me.

Lauren Bacall

I was thrilled when I heard I was going to Africa to make a movie. I'm always thrilled to be going somewhere exotic. I didn't want to leave our son, but Bogey convinced me that it would be another great adventure with Huston. We just hoped that we would get out alive, since John always chose such remote locations. There was some malaria and dysentery among the crew, but I never got sick, nor did Bogey or John. We had to shut down production for a few days when half the crew were so ill, out in the jungle with swarming insects and leeches in the river. I was playing Florence Nightingale, walking around in the infirmary, asking how everyone was, and if there was something I could get for them.

Katie and I became very good friends on that trip, but I didn't know her at all before we met in London. She was alone, which obviously is difficult for anyone to be, especially on an African location like that. But she loves adventure, as I do, and Africa was an exciting place to be going. Our lives were not seriously threatened, but the illness was not easy. Bogey and John and I were the only ones who didn't get sick at all. Once Katie got dysentery, because she took a chance and drank the wrong kind of water. I even brushed my teeth in bottled water. I've always been very meticulous. Bogey and John never took a drink until the end of the day, and in Africa you can't drink a lot at night and get up ready to work at six in the morning. One drink is like five in Africa. You have to be very careful in that climate, where a drink affects you much more. It's like being at high altitude. I never have been a big drinker, and they certainly weren't drunk every night, so I think they were lucky. Whatever water we drank was bottled.

Olivia de Havilland

John Huston loved life, and he had so much of it, was so full of it, that he could spend it recklessly. He always had tremendous vigor of every kind, intellectual included. He directed Bette and me in 1942 in *In This Our Life*, and he became one of my great friends. He was quite a fellow. Isn't it wonderful how he kept on doing splendid things? He gave up his castle in Ireland a long time ago, and lived until the end in his villa in Mexico. The climate was better for him, for he needed the heat rather than the cold. He had terrible emphysema, but an extraordinary constitution, and he remained active and productive and creative, and probably reckless, too, until he died.

George C. Scott

I made two pictures with John Huston, *The List of Adrian Messenger* in 1963 and *The Bible* in 1966, and we started out doing *The Last Run* together, but we had to fire Huston on that one. That dear man had emphysema so bad he couldn't breathe. He got his breath through a tube affair—and I'm not far behind him, I'll tell you. I suck oxygen every night. I keep an oxygen tent in my dressing room, whenever I'm working. I can't stop smoking, though I did once for eight months.

Audrey Hepburn

I think that John Huston's record shows him to be one of the very greatest directors. He was a very funny man, a real character, always very jovial and warmhearted and full of stories. He was a real storyteller, in fact, and very interesting to be with.

He directed me with Burt Lancaster in *The Unforgiven* in 1960, and I broke my back falling off a horse in that one. It was no joke. I was in a brace for quite a while, and in fact I'm very lucky to be here at all, much less moving around. If the break had been any higher I would have been paralyzed. I spent four months in the hospital, because I had been riding up a storm on a magnificent horse, one of them that was not used to all the shenanigans on a movie set. I think he belonged to a dentist. He got spooked and threw me, and I landed on a rock. That gave me not only a concussion; it broke all the bones in my back. I had to be taken back to L.A. in an ambulance plane, and I lay there for five weeks.

As soon as I could walk I was back on the set, and I finished the picture. Fortunately, most of *The Unforgiven* had already been shot by that point, so you can't tell that anything has happened. I could no longer ride a horse, for I was unable to mount and dismount. It was just impossible for me to pull myself up into the saddle or even get my toe into the stirrup, for I had no strength at all in my back after the break. But I still had to complete several horse scenes, so they fixed up a box and lifted me onto the horse for those.

Gregory Peck

I made *Moby Dick* with John Huston in 1956, and that was quite an experience, too. I was scared to death, tied to a white rubber whale out in the Irish Sea. We were out there pitching and tossing in bad weather, unable to film anything, and for anyone who had not been on the boat in those seas before it was certain seasickness the minute you stepped aboard. Oh, my God, the damned thing was doing up and down in heavy seas. We got used to it, though, so we sat around below deck and played poker with stormy skies overhead.

We were supposed to be in the South Pacific, where the whalers used to go to harpoon the whales. They never went to the Irish Sea! But we were there because John wanted to be close to his home in Ireland. The conditions were very uncomfortable, and as a matter of fact I could have died very easily making *Moby Dick*. This rubber whale broke loose in very bad weather and immediately got separated from the boats in the fog. We were probably damned fools to be out there trying to get the shot in the first place.

But I drifted off, tied to this huge white whale in very choppy seas, with waves at least eight feet slapping against the whale. I was slithering around on top of this rubber whale, hanging on to the ropes and the harpoons that were stuck into him, completely out of sight of everybody. I had no idea where the camera launch and the tow launch were. I couldn't see ten feet in that fog, and I thought, "Oh, my God, I'm going to die, tied to the back of a rubber whale out in the middle of the Irish Sea!" I became very calm when I realized that there was no hope for me, and I thought of the headlines in the papers: "Gregory Peck Dies on the Back of a Whale," or "Actor Lost at Sea." It was kind of funny, I guess. I thought of my folks at home during the ten minutes that I was absolutely helpless out there. If I had somehow slipped into the sea I wouldn't have known which direction either Ireland or Wales was in, and I might have started to swim toward the South Pole. I was completely disoriented in this thick fog.

Suddenly I remembered that Hemingway had said that when you feel physical fear, and know that your life is in danger, you get queasy in the stomach, followed by a weakness in the legs. He must have known this from the bullring. Well, I felt queasy and weak, and I was yelling "Here I am! Where are you? Camera launch!" After ten minutes the camera launch appeared out of the fog and nudged up against the whale, so I slid down the side of Moby Dick into the launch. It could have been a stupid misadventure ending in my death. It might make a funny story, but at the time I wasn't laughing, even though it did occur to me that it was a funny way to die. But it was not the way I had planned to go. After I got away from Moby Dick he sailed away and was never seen again. Perhaps even today there is a great white rubber whale swimming the Irish Sea. Huston was determined that nothing would stand in the way of completing his movies.

James Stewart

Billy Wilder also refused to let difficulties get him down. He would just go on to the next scene, and he came very well prepared. *The Spirit of St. Louis* was a very difficult picture to make, with long aerial shots and everything else, but Billy was certainly the right director for that one. It's amazing to me to learn the number of people who see that one on television. It was kept off the tube for a long time.

You may recall that after I took off from Newfoundland there was a fly in the cockpit. Well, that fly was Billy's idea. I recall getting a little annoyed with the fly, and I told him that as we got over the ocean we should get rid of the fly, for the thing was difficult enough to do without this bug buzzing around in my face. Billy and I got into a bit of an argument about the fly at that point, and Leland Hayward, who was producing *The Spirit of St. Louis*, was the only one to see my side of the argument. Now there really wasn't too much that I could do to make the long segment of my flight across the Atlantic all that interesting, so Billy wanted to keep the fly.

We finally finished the film and it opened in Radio City Music Hall in New York while I was on a fishing trip with friends in Chile and Argentina, and we were in a little hotel in Brazil after going up the Amazon. I got a phone call from New York, and the man on the other end said, "This is Charles Lindbergh. I just saw the picture, and it seemed to me to go very well. By the way, thanks for getting rid of the fly."

James Cagney

In 1961 I made *One, Two, Three* with Billy Wilder, and it was the film that convinced me to retire from show business. We were making that picture in Berlin inside a dark studio. I walked outside into the beautiful sunshine, and decided right then that that was it. The thought of stopping was so wonderful that I resolved then that it would be my last film. Of course, I went back to work later on, surprising everyone by agreeing to play Rhinelander Waldo, the police commissioner in *Ragtime*. It was my friend Carroll O'Connor who suggested that I get Milos Forman to enlarge the role for me, and he was willing. The rest is history. Pat O'Brien was in that picture, too, and I was happy to be working with him again. Since the Morgan Library wouldn't let us shoot the outdoor scene there we had to go to England. It was just as well, for I got to meet the Queen Mother at the London Palladium then.

Audrey Hepburn

Billy Wilder directed me twice, in *Sabrina* as well as in *Love in the Afternoon*, which we made in 1957 with Gary Cooper. The marvelous thing about Billy is his wit. It just goes on all day long, and frankly I think that it is the best way to work. Keeping everyone laughing and happy and amused is the best way to get good performances out of actors, I think. It puts you in a good mood, and if you're relaxed you can do a much better job, I find.

I think that Billy knew exactly what he was getting into with *Love in the Afternoon*. It was taken from a book called *Ariane*, by Claude Anet, in which an eighteen-year-old girl falls in love with a much older man. In the film he was an American millionaire, and ironically he was being investigated by the father of the girl, who was played by Maurice Chevalier. She tried to live up to the experience without the benefit of any experience at all, and that was intended to appeal to women. Today it would certainly not cause moral consternation, but back then we were met with indignation at this love affair between a young girl and an old man.

Jack Lemmon

Billy Wilder had seen some of the films I had made, particularly the two with Judy Holliday, *It Should Happen to You* and *Phffft*, and he had decided that he wanted me for *Some*

Like It Hot. When he got Marilyn and Tony he knew that he had enough firepower, so to speak, to hold out for me. Actually, a lot of people wanted that role, including Frank Sinatra and Danny Kaye.

One night before Felicia Farr and I were married we were having dinner in Dominique's, a little restaurant in Hollywood, and Billy walked up to me. He said that he wanted to speak to me, so on the way out I stopped by his table, and in just a few words he explained the plot to me: "These two guys witness the St. Valentine's Day massacre, and they have to hide, so they dress up as girls and join a traveling female orchestra. Three-quarters of the film you and Tony will have to be in drag. Do you want the part?" he asked. "Yes, yes, yes," I answered, and that was that. The idea of it all was funny, to be sure, but I decided to do it because it was a Billy Wilder film.

I knew that I would be taking a chance on it, but by the second week of shooting I realized that I was involved in something very special. It was an absolute hoot to make, and there was never any fear about the quality of it, or the taste of it, which might have been a real problem. It was a delicate situation, but worth the risk. I had no idea that it would prove to be such a hit, and a classic.

I remember that in *Some Like It Hot* we had a twenty-minute conference before I was permitted to make one change, and that was only an addition. Early on in the film there is a scene in which Tony and I are talking to a booking agent, who offers us a little gig over in New Jersey. My line was "Now you're talking!" I asked Billy if I could say, "Now you are talking," and it took nearly a half hour to get that change approved, as if the script was the Bible. It's kind of like trying to improve upon Shakespeare by ad-libbing. You'll just screw it up if you try to change a Billy Wilder script.

When I was making *The Apartment* with Shirley MacLaine I learned that you don't change a single comma in a Billy Wilder script. Shirley was a delight to work with, a human bubble three feet off the ground, with a lot of energy, and just terrific. She was not as disciplined as Billy would have liked, however, so that ended in about three days. You see, Shirley likes to work by getting a pretty good idea of the script, and then letting it all come naturally. So, he waited, and I could see the look in his eye as Shirley was going along, doing her own thing. She hadn't worked with him before, but I had, and so she was screwing around with her lines.

Billy waited until she had a long monologue in an elevator, where she was the elevator operator, and people were getting on and off. He was shooting the entire scene in one take, and every time that she changed one word, "the" or "and," Billy would shout, "Cut!" He had the script right next to him, and he followed it closely. Well, she did that sucker about thirty times, and could never get all the way through the two pages of monologue without changing some little word and having Billy stop it. Finally she got tired of having to redo it, so she gave up and did it word perfect, and that cured her. She never took the liberty of changing another word in the entire script.

The three of us worked together again several years later on *Irma La Douce*. I remember that one vividly, because Felicia and I got married when we were going over to Europe to film it. After we shot the few location scenes there we were to have a hiatus of a few days, so we decided that it would be a great place for a honeymoon. So, the morning after we were married I had a five o'clock call to get to makeup, and then by seven that morning I was coming out of the Seine, which is polluted. They had to put a rubber suit on me, but some of the water got into my mouth, and I spent the rest of my honeymoon with the worst case of dysentery on record. But that was about all we shot in Paris, just what they really needed for exteriors. Everything else was filmed on the lot back in Los Angeles, where they built that whole little area of Paris.

James Stewart

Without any doubt Frank Capra was the greatest director I ever knew. I have the utmost respect and admiration for him. He was able to do things like no one else, there's no question about it. He had a very solid sense of values, real values, like flag and family and friends, and community, and God, and because of his remarkable gift for humor he was able to get all of those values into his pictures without ever appearing to preach. It was almost like magic when you saw it happening.

The combination of truth and humor in his films always works, and never seems dated, for he was making pictures about universal experience, and there was something very special indeed about his talent. He was always so subtle, yet so accurate. He would set things up in such a way that as an actor you would be almost surprised that things were going so well, and so quickly. Before you knew it the scene was over and Capra would say, "Fine!"

As I think back I recall no rehearsals like you had in the theater, in which the actors would go through a scene under the director's supervision for him to observe and then decide what he wanted to do. No one rehearsed to make a movie back in those days. You knew your lines, as did everyone else, and then you shot the scene, doing the best you could, though sometimes you would have to reshoot it.

It's a Wonderful Life is my favorite picture, as well as Frank Capra's personal favorite. In a way here again is an example of the tremendous good fortune I've had. I had been away for four years, and this was the first part I got when I returned from the war. I wasn't sure that it was right for me, or that I was right for it. Frank wasn't sure either, for I hadn't done any acting since 1941, and he hadn't been making this kind of picture for a while either. He had been in the Army making films like *Why We Fight* for the government to boost morale. So, at the start of *It's a Wonderful Life* neither one of us was sure, but it didn't take us long to get into the spirit of the picture when we started shooting it, because Capra had that rare ability to get his values over with humor. It's amazing to consider the people who were in that picture: Lionel Barrymore, Donna Reed, Henry Travers, Thomas Mitchell, Beulah Bondi, Frank Faylen, Gloria Grahame, and many others. Every one of them was perfectly cast.

I like to think that I have never lost sight of something that

Ted Healy told me back in 1936, when I was filming *Speed*. He was the straight man for the Three Stooges when they were in vaudeville, and he said, "You know, you may do all right out here. It's kind of a rough racket, but you may make it. But there's one thing I want you to remember always, and that is that you must never treat your audience as customers. You must always treat them as partners." I've never forgotten that, for it was one of the true pearls of wisdom I always remember about the responsibility of an actor. So, I always paid attention to this job I had, which was acting, and I never loafed around.

I do feel that I was successful in developing an acting style that made it possible for the acting as such not to show, which is very important. If you have people in the audience believing what you're doing, then you're getting somewhere, because believability starts to sneak in when the acting doesn't show. The actor needs to believe what he is doing, too, and to develop a confidence in what he is doing or saying, whether it is one line or a long speech, as I had to do in *Mr. Smith Goes to Washington*. The decisions you make about how to deliver a given line are important, but whatever you decide you must have full confidence in your decisions.

Hank Fonda could read two pages just once and put it down, having effortlessly memorized the entire thing. He could recite the whole thing without making a single mistake. That is a gift, I think. He had total recall, as did Humphrey Bogart. As for me, and especially as George Bailey, it was a matter of having my acting seem believable. The story might or might not be realistic, but credibility is the bottom line. That is what I have tried to achieve through the years.

I am told that *It's a Wonderful Life* has been played more than any other film in the history of movies, and one reason for that is that it fell into the public domain when the copyright was not renewed, which was just an oversight. The picture didn't do any business when it was released; it was a terrible flop. You see, Frank Capra had formed Liberty Pictures with Willie Wyler and George Stevens and Sam Briskin.

Each one of them had a film that he wanted to make, but they all wanted Frank to make *It's a Wonderful Life* as their first venture, since all of them were so sure that it would be a critical hit and a big money-maker. Well, it not only failed commercially and critically, it broke the company. Liberty Pictures went into bankruptcy and was unable to go forward and make any more films. In selling their assets to Paramount they forgot to renew the copyright, so through an oversight *It's a Wonderful Life* went into the public domain.

Douglas Fairbanks, Jr.

Frank Capra was just beginning at the time we were together, so he was not then known as a great director. I remember him fondly, and we got along very well, but I don't think that either one of us recognized in the other any great future. I was simply a leading man trying to keep my career going, and he was making his second picture. It was called *The Power of the Press*, and it came out in 1928. We remained friends, but never worked together again.

James Stewart

Like all of the greatest directors, Frank Capra let you work things out for yourself. Most of them had wonderful judgment, so they were looking at you as a part of an ensemble in order to get a whole picture. You looked at the job as a question of how to make your character grow within the confines of the story, the conflict, the relations with the other parts.

I think that the reason most of the best-known actors and actresses were successful is that they had personalities that translated well into screen personas. Audiences knew what they were going to get when they went to a film starring Errol Flynn, or Bette Davis, or Greta Garbo, or Gary Cooper. Frank always had the story so well set in his mind that there was never any problem of what to do, and in that sense he was like so many of the good ones, like John Ford and Henry Hathaway.

In my case, he wanted me to be myself, to play the role as Jimmy Stewart, whether it was in *It's a Wonderful Life* or *Mr. Smith Goes to Washington*. In that one, I had an awful lot to say, in that filibuster, and it had to be fast, which meant I had to know the lines cold. I've always had a terrible time learning lines. Now for the effect on the screen my throat had to get sore, so one night Capra came down and said to me, "You know, you don't convince me that your throat is sore. It sounds like you're just trying to make it sound as if your voice is giving out."

This worried me, so that night I stopped by the office of an ear, nose, and throat doctor whom I knew in Brentwood. I asked him if there was any way that he could give me a sore throat. Well, he just sat and looked at me for a moment, and then he said, "I've heard that you Hollywood actors are crazy, but you take the cake. It's taken me thirty years to learn how to keep people from getting sore throats, and to cure them when they've got one. Now you come in and want me to give you a sore throat! Well, I'll give you the sorest throat you ever had!" He then took a couple of drops of bichloride of mercury and put them on my vocal cords. Well, I could hardly swallow. "Is that what you mean?" he asked. I nodded, then rasped out, "Can you give me some of that so that I can administer it when needed?" "No, a doctor has to apply this. But you've got me so fascinated with this that I'll see you tomorrow morning at nine o'clock on the set," he suggested. I don't know what happened to his patients, but he was there at nine, and he stayed for the whole day. Every once in a while I would come over to him to tell him that it was getting better, so he would administer a little more, and my voice would sound like I had been talking for days. I've often felt that this type of technique wouldn't go over well with the Actors Studio, with method acting. It was painful.

Loretta Young

I loved Frank Capra, and he was just darling to me. He was a charming, gentle man, as well as one of the great directors. We were making *Platinum Blonde* back in 1931 with Jean Harlow, and he said to me, "Now, Loretta, what do you think about this?" I replied to him, "Oh, Mr. Capra, it doesn't make any difference what I think. You just tell me what you want me to do, and I'll try to do it." He gave me a funny look and said, "But Loretta, that's all acting is: thinking." Well, from then on the whole world opened up for me, and God help any director who told me simply to do something. I would argue that I thought this or that.

Frank was quite right, and Harlow was darling, too. I never got to know her too well, but what I do know is not at all like the books I've read about her indicate. If she had slept around so much she wouldn't have had any time to make films. In her way she probably was one of the "modern" ones, like the girls are today, and she lived by her own standards. They certainly weren't like mine, but we are what we are, and you really can't ask any more of someone than to be what he or she is. If they call me "strong-willed," that's tough. Sorry! Can you imagine how far you would get in this business by being Miss Mush? Not far at all.

Katharine Hepburn

Jean Harlow was a damned good actress who made all those men seem fascinating. But she had died by the time I was on the Metro lot.

Carroll Baker

In 1965, after I had been cast as Jean Harlow, I was supposed to ride through the golden gates of Paramount in an antique

Jean Harlow, *Dinner at Eight*, 1933

Carroll Baker, *Harlow*, 1965

car, and this was the first time in twenty-five years that the gates had been opened.

Well, I was dressed up like Harlow herself, in a very heavy beaded dress, and I had two very large Russian wolfhounds that were hard to manage, and I was wearing an oversized white fox stole. They managed to get me, in this heavy dress and huge fur, into the backseat of the car with both dogs, and it really wasn't my fault: there simply was not enough room for Joe Levine, who was quite a large man, and I was cooperating with this publicity stunt, looking like Harlow and struggling with the two dogs. Someone at Paramount told him that there was nothing they could do to fit him into the car, and that since everyone was waiting they had better open the gates and let me go through.

So, I ended up riding through the golden gates of Paramount without Joe Levine, and from that day on he never spoke to me again. From then on he did everything possible to kill the film, and he gave us none of the resources we needed, and he rushed us into production without adequate preparation. He even refused to give John Michael Hayes the time he wanted to do the needed rewrites on the script, for everyone was laughing about the dialogue. He gave us no time to rehearse, so that Peter Lawford, Angela Lansbury, Raf Vallone, Red Buttons, and myself would all have to stay after work to go over our lines for the next day. It was either that or rehearse during the lunch break or come in early in the morning. He treated us all so poorly, trying to make *Harlow* fail by forcing us to go in front of the camera without ever having had the chance to run through our lines together. Going through the action cold with the camera rolling is a terrible experience, I can tell you.

I didn't become ill or die like Jean Harlow, but I did refuse to be treated with so little consideration, so the studio decided that they would make an example of me, since they felt they couldn't afford to have actresses going around having their own way while they were under contract. So, they blocked all the money I had made on *Harlow*, and I had to go to the Screen Actors Guild to see the president, Charlton Heston, who was a friend, and tell him how they were starving me out. They hadn't even paid me my salary for *Harlow*, which had been completed over a year earlier. They had a special meeting of the officers of SAG, and Heston pleaded my case, so SAG managed to get my money for me. But I knew that I wouldn't be able to get work for a long time, and I decided to move to Europe. I never got it in writing that I was being blackballed, but I did have a very good theatrical agency that was trying to get work for me, and they finally came to me and said, "Well, Carroll, we think you're being black-balled, because no one will hire you." *Harlow* was basically the end of my American film career.

James Stewart

In 1936 I played Jean Harlow's boyfriend in *Wife Versus Secretary*, and I will never forget the good-bye kiss we had before she left me for Clark Gable, who was married to Myrna Loy in that one. She was a very good kisser, to say the least, and it was really a new experience for me to be kissed like that. Here again, it was a lucky break for me to be cast in a small role in a picture with a lot of big stars.

Loretta Young

I loved Jimmy Stewart from the first time I saw him. He's a charming man, and he's fortunate in having an unusual woman as his wife. But I was crazy about Jimmy, and dated him a lot, but I guess the Lord said no to that one. I don't know what happened. He's been married to Gloria all these years, while so many people around him have been divorced and had multiple marriages. Actually, I was dating Tom Lewis at the same time I dated Jimmy, so I guess you could say I'm kind of a frivolous one in that way, being so crazy about so many men.

Olivia de Havilland

I think I met Jimmy Stewart immediately after we finished filming *Gone With the Wind*. As a matter of fact, I had to go back to reshoot some scenes in *Gone With the Wind* after I had already begun *The Private Lives of Elizabeth and Essex*, which was starring Bette Davis and Errol Flynn. That was a dreadfully difficult thing to do, to shift back and forth between those two roles, one in Atlanta in the Civil War, and the other in Renaissance England.

Maybe it was when I was making *Santa Fe Trail* that I was seeing Jimmy. In any case, isn't it a pity that we never made a movie together? I mean there were films in which we both appeared, like *Airport '77*, but we never had any scenes together in it.

We first met in New York City at the end of 1939, and it had to do with the opening of *Gone With the Wind* there. Howard Hughes wanted some friend of his to escort me to the opening, and I told Irene Selznick about it. She said to me, "That will never do! He's nothing but an old roué! We cannot have that, so we've got to think of better casting." So she arranged everything for me. She got hold of Leland Hayward, and told him that Jimmy Stewart would be just right for me, since he had just done *Mr. Smith Goes to Washington*. Leland agreed that Jimmy would thus be the perfect one to escort me to the New York opening of *Gone With the Wind*. Jimmy and I had never met, but he came to pick me up at the airport in this long limousine on a cold day. He was wearing a long navy-blue coat with a hat. I got into the car and sat on the right side and we never said a word, because both of us were so shy. It was like a contest of shyness, with him on the left.

There are photographs of the two of us going into the theater that night. He is an awfully nice guy. I stayed on in New York a little bit, and he invited me to a matinee, and to supper afterward. I remember saying in my timid, breathless way that I thought that would be a good idea, so one day we went to a lovely play, and afterward met a friend of Jimmy's from Princeton. The play was *Morning's At Seven*, and I think Dorothy Gish was in it. The director was Josh Logan, and that's when I met him. There were very few people in the theater, but everyone there became friends, since the play was so beautiful.

Joan Fontaine

I made *You Gotta Stay Happy* with Jimmy Stewart in 1948, and I had a potential miscarriage while filming it with him. That dear man was the only one who came to see me in the hospital. Not long ago we were together at the Berlin Film Festival, and the two of us were sitting side by side being interviewed. We just looked at each other, knowing all that had happened—the good fortune, the grief, the good times, the misery, the success, the pain—and without saying anything we just put our arms around each other and had a silent hug. There was no need to say anything. There was nothing *to* say. We had gotten this far through it all, and it was not an easy path. But he, too, is a survivor, as was dear Henry Fonda. *On Golden Pond* was among Hank's finest performances. As an actor he was not diminished by age.

Carroll Baker

When you genuinely love people and admire them and think that they are just so great, what can you say? Working with Jimmy Stewart was a joy for me. We met on the set of *How the West Was Won*, and the segments we did together involved some difficult physical exertion. On location he and Debbie Reynolds and I were stuck in a cave after a landslide, and we had to sit there for several hours telling each other jokes until we could be rescued, and this was not part of the script—it really happened. He and Debbie both have remained dear friends of mine, and maybe the cave had something to do with it, although I did marry him in that movie.

Once Jimmy did something for me that was very special. It was one of those Foreign Press Award dinners in Los Angeles where I was supposed to stand up and receive an award for one of Joe Levine's films. I've forgotten which film it was, but I had just come in from Paris, wearing what I suppose was the very first evening slacks suit seen in America. It came from the House of Pierre Balmain, and it was all colored sequins, and quite striking. When I stood up to accept the award this buzz went through the audience, for it was considered absolutely scandalous that any lady would dare to wear pants to a Hollywood awards ceremony.

Well, after you accepted the award you were supposed to go backstage to be photographed with everyone else in that category. When I went up onto the ramp to be photographed with the other winners they all disappeared, for no one wanted to be seen in the company of a woman in pants. So, there I was, standing alone with egg on my face, and the photographers didn't know what to do. Jimmy Stewart had been in another category, but when he saw that I was left there all alone he made a long and circuitous route to come all the way back in and get up onto the platform with me. "I think she looks beautiful," he announced to the press, "and I want to have my picture taken with her."

George C. Scott

Jimmy Stewart was great to me, too. Class, man, if ever there was one with it, and that's why he's been a major star for fifty years. We played the opposing lawyers in the courtroom in Otto Preminger's *Anatomy of a Murder* in 1959, and we would do the close-ups first, starting with his. Then we reversed it, and since I had a lot of close-ups, he was to be off-camera. They called him to the set to deliver his lines to me, and I noticed that he was in his shirtsleeves, with no tie and no vest. "Would you come over here, Mr. Stewart, to give Mr. Scott your line?" they said to him. So, he stood up, rolled down his sleeves, buttoned his cuffs, put on his tie, then his vest, and then his jacket, and was in complete costume to look me in the eye and give me his lines for my close-up. I said to myself at the time, "That's a class act, and I will always do that for other people," and I have. I will never do an off-camera line unless I'm in full costume, so the other actor can see me as I'm supposed to be, as the character I'm playing. It's a matter of courtesy.

Jimmy Stewart is a bloody champion among gentlemen, as was Gary Cooper. Coop was one of the sweetest men I ever met. He died just two years after completion of the picture I made with him, called *The Hanging Tree*. He had cancer of the prostate when we shot it, in 1958, so he couldn't mount a horse at that point, and he made only one more picture after that, I think. He was a big, easy, gentle man, and everyone loved him. He had hands the size of hams. He was a cartoonist for a Montana newspaper, and all he ever wanted to be was an artist. Slim Talbot was his stuntman and double for years, and he had gotten sick of cattle ranching back in the early twenties. So he headed for Hollywood, liked it, and sent Coop a wire saying, "Come on down! We've got it made here! They need wranglers and all kinds of things we can do!" Slim got Coop his first job, and was with him off and on for thirty years or more. They were like brothers. When I see one of Coop's films now I can always tell who's riding the horse, because Slim always rode with his elbows out, and Coop never did. They were lovely people.

Coop was so kind to me, because *The Hanging Tree* was my first film, and I had to play a drunken faith healer in it named George Grubb. I'll never forget the first day of shooting. I had this huge theological harangue to deliver to the mob. Oh, I was terrified! It was about a page and a half long, and I was so scared I couldn't even recall my own name, much less the lines.

Coop, like all of us, was married several times, and his last wife, Rocky, was with him when he died. And that was back in 1960. I don't think I ever heard anyone say anything bad about Gary Cooper.

Helen Hayes

I made *A Farewell to Arms* with Gary Cooper in 1932, and it was a great picture. I had a bit of a crush on him, but I don't think he ever knew it. And if he had, nothing would have come of it.

I knew that Gary was a cartoonist with a newspaper, but I never knew that he had done any rough stuff. My goodness, you couldn't get much rougher than being a cattle hand. I always found him to be so gentle. In fact, he was rather aesthetic, and never revealed anything that would have led me to think he had been a stuntman. I wonder if that really is true.

But then such crazy stories get around about everybody in Hollywood. It was the greatest gossip mill there ever was. When I was doing *A Farewell to Arms* at Paramount, on loan-out from MGM, mind you, Marlene Dietrich was there making *The Scarlet Empress* with Josef von Sternberg. You see, the first film I made was sort of a sex picture, *The Sin of Madelon Claudet*, which my husband Charlie had written. Actually, I won the Oscar as Best Actress for it. My next picture was *Arrowsmith*, based on the Sinclair Lewis novel, opposite Ronald Colman, which Sam Goldwyn produced. And then came *A Farewell to Arms* at Paramount, where I got to know Marlene.

I recall that she had to get to the studio early in the morning, since she was having her hair sprayed with gold dust. In fact, she was having the most complete makeup job I have ever seen on anyone, from the top of her head to the soles of her feet. It took hours to get her together for the cameras, and this was very early in the morning. But before she came to the studio she cooked an entire lunch for Maria, her daughter, who would be taken off to school by the nursemaid, then brought back home for a hot lunch. Marlene, being the good

Gary Cooper, ca. 1934

German *Frau*, actually prepared her daughter's lunch each day before going to work, because she didn't want Maria eating a cold lunch in a delicatessen or even going into a restaurant. Of course, the lunch the school provided was utterly out of the question for Maria. She had to have good, hot, wholesome German lunches. So, Marlene would cook this big lunch and leave it on the stove, then dash off to the studio, where she always brought a portion of what she had fixed to give to me. She fed me as well as her daughter. She was such a darling, and I loved her so dearly.

Our friendship continued for many years, too. When my own daughter Mary died of polio Marlene was so sympathetic. By an ironic twist of fate, Marlene's daughter Maria had a child who also came down with polio. Then it was announced all over the world that Dr. Jonas Salk had finally developed a vaccine for polio that had been proven effective, and that very morning, at eight o'clock, I received a phone call from Marlene: "Halloo, Helen. I am so very happy, and I know what this means to you," she said in that soft, low voice.

Marlene and Norma Shearer and Mary Pickford were all goddesses, creatures of such beauty that they just couldn't bear to be seen in anything less than top form, which is pretty hard when you're sixty or more. Heavens, I'm over ninety.

Loretta Young

Dear old Gary. I made *Along Came Jones* with him in 1945, and I knew him so well as a social friend that we got along very easily at work. He was a young Adonis when I first knew him, and his daughter went to the same school as mine, and his wife, Rocky, and I were very friendly, too.

As charming as he was, though, I did not care for the shy, "Charlie Ray" persona that he carried around. I don't know if it was his true character, or if he assumed it, but that little-boy stuff did not appeal to me. Frankly, I never found him very stimulating, but then I was never in a situation where he had to be anything other than polite and nice.

On the film we made he was very hard of hearing, which he never told anyone, and it embarrassed people when they would talk to him and he would either not look at them or give them the wrong answer. It made you look like an idiot. Coop never did tell many people that he was as deaf as a post in one ear, and it could have saved a lot of embarrassment. One day the assistant director came and said, "Mr. Cooper, we're ready for you now." Gary was looking at me, and this nice young man was there on his other side, but Gary kept on talking to me, since he didn't hear him. Finally I said, "Gary, you've got company." Well, Gary just looked at the guy and kept on talking to me for at least another half a minute, so finally I had to tell Gary that they were ready for him.

Later on I suggested to Gary that he hang a sign on his chest that said, "Yell at me—I'm hard-of-hearing." He tried to hush me up about it, but I insisted that he do something about it, if he didn't want to wear a hearing aid. I'm glad that I had that little experience with Gary, because when I started to lose my hearing I told the priest at mass that he would have to speak up and stop mumbling, so my mother sent me down to see the doctor, who told me that I had lost twenty percent of my hearing in one ear. Dear old Coop. I think the men were more interested in him than the women, because he was such a role model.

James Stewart

Gary and Rocky gave the dinner party where I met my wife Gloria, and we have all remained very good friends, long after Gary's death. I was seated next to Gloria at that dinner, and then I asked if I could take her home afterward, which I did. She had bought a new place up in Bel-Air after her divorce, where she was living with her two boys. When we got to the door of this little house I asked for the key, and when I opened the door a huge German shepherd bared his teeth and was about to lunge at my throat when Gloria, in a soft tone like you would use for a baby, told him to be quiet. He calmed down right away and left us alone. "Would you like to come in for a drink?" she offered, but I was so shaken by this ferocious dog that I declined and quickly left.

This started us off, though, and we began to play golf quite a lot, but every time I took her home that dog would act like he was going to rip my throat out. I was, of course, getting pretty stuck on her, but I knew that I was never going to get her without getting the dog, too. I tried everything—going to the pet store and buying little toys and treats, searching for the finest things to pacify him. I remember one Saturday after we had played eighteen holes Gloria said to me, "You know, I eat, too." Well, this is where Chasen's came in, so our courtship was sort of between the golf course and Dave Chasen's restaurant. Then one night after several months of our dating, the dog finally came in and put his head down on my lap. I patted him, and we were at last friends. I guess I have Gary Cooper to thank, in part at least, for my more than forty years of happy marriage.

James Cagney

Not long ago Joel McCrea told a story about standing around on a set with Gary Cooper, back during the war, when they got word that someone was waiting in the wings to see them. So, they walked over, expecting to see a beautiful girl, and there I was. I wanted to ask them if they would be willing to go to Europe to do something for the war effort, and they both said, "Anything for you!" It made me feel wonderful to have such loyal friends who felt the same way I did about supporting our country in her time of greatest need.

Anyway, they were walking out of the studio, when Bob Hope saw them and said, "Hey, where are you two going?" "We're going over to Europe for Cagney!" Gary answered. Hope then asked, "What are you going to do over there? You can't sing or dance." So Gary replied, "We're gonna put up a screen and show our pictures to the troops!"

Rossano Brazzi

Gary Cooper was a wonderful man. When I was in Hawaii making *South Pacific*, Gary and Rocky would call me in Kauai to ask when we were coming back to Hollywood, so that they could plan a party for us. We had planned on spending two and a half months there, but it took more than four months to film it all. After we at last completed the filming we returned to Hollywood, and Gary hosted a tremendous dinner party in my honor. That is what I mean by solidarity among the old-time Hollywood stars, what they call "Hollywood Royalty." In Italy there is nothing at all like this. There is no solidarity at all among Italian actors, because they all hate each other. It is rivalry and jealousy and competition, as opposed to a spirit of camaraderie. Maybe that no longer exists in Hollywood, either. I don't know.

Rod Steiger

Gary Cooper was a sweetheart, and I had the honor of acting with him in Otto Preminger's *The Court-Martial of Billy Mitchell*. That was kind of a funny situation in itself, for everyone had been telling me to watch out for Otto, that he was a monster. In fact, they couldn't wait to see what happened when the two of us got together, since they all expected the sparks to fly for thirty miles.

So, I went onto the set, introduced myself to him, and just stood there. "I know who you are," he responded. "So what are we going to do?" I asked. "This is the way I see the character, Mr. Steiger," he started in that heavy German accent of his. He went on for about twenty minutes, lecturing me about how I needed to understand that this man wanted to make more out of himself. When he concluded his analysis he asked what I had to say about it, so I responded by imitating his own voice and accent: "By Christ, Otto, if that's the way you want to play the part then that's the way we'll play the goddamned character!" He fell in love with me on the spot, and after that I could do nothing wrong in his eyes. If in the middle of a scene I would scratch my ear he would want to stop so that we could shoot a close-up. "No, Otto, I did that because it itched. It didn't mean anything," I would have to insist.

I believe that I have the distinction of having participated in Gary Cooper's only public performance, which was on "The Ed Sullivan Show." They wanted to get some publicity for *Billy Mitchell*, so they talked Coop into doing this live TV show. He said that he would do the scene only if Rod Steiger did it with him, which was awfully nice of him. So, we did the scene on live TV, and it was the first time I saw the perspiration of an actor dripping out of his sleeves onstage. That's how nervous he was. He got lost once or twice, but we got back on track. I said to him, "Just listen to me and think, 'Do you really believe that bombs can sink a battleship?' "

I've learned that whenever you hear an actor say, "Don't look at me! I know what you're trying to tell me!" you can be sure that he's lost. Coop was supposed to say that "Charlie" was trying to take over the East Side, but instead I had to say it for him and make it look as if everything still added up. Live television is the worst medium ever invented, but it was also the most exciting. You had the pressure of an opening night, with only one shot at it, and at the same time you were within the confines of the movie set.

Gregory Peck

One of my regrets is that I turned down an offer to do *High Noon*, so it went to Gary Cooper, and he won the Oscar for it. I definitely made a misjudgment on that one, but the extenuating circumstance was that I thought I had already played the part in *The Gunfighter*. Those two films were made within a year of each other, and my work in *The Gunfighter* was the reason that Stanley Kramer asked me to do *High Noon*. I was an outlaw, rather than a sheriff, but still I was a man against the town, with no one to help him but himself. I probably read the script hurriedly and said that it was too much like *The Gunfighter*, and that I didn't want to do the same thing twice, which was a case of misplaced idealism, I suppose. On the other hand, I did do about ten westerns, even though I never wanted to be a cowboy actor. I remember that Duke Wayne used to talk about having passed up *Twelve O'Clock High*, for which I won the New York Film Critics' Award, so you see, we all make mistakes.

Audrey Hepburn

Gary Cooper had absolutely beautiful eyes, like brilliant sapphires, and his daughter Maria has them as well. Gary was so sweet and dear, such a total gentleman. At the end of filming *Love in the Afternoon* he left me his lighter to remember him, and I was so touched. I remember going to see him just before he died, and he was so brave. He was suffering so terribly with the cancer, but he died with his boots on, as they say, with such courage.

Lauren Bacall

I made *Bright Leaf* with Gary Cooper in 1950 because I was quite obviously longing to work with him. He was a very fine actor, and to this day unfairly underrated. What a great-looking guy, and what beautiful blue eyes! He had the bluest eyes of anyone I have ever seen. They were absolutely cornflower blue. I have never seen such heavenly eyes again in my life, including Paul Newman's. They were just electric, staggering. And Gary was so tall and handsome. The men liked him, and the ladies liked him, and he sure liked the ladies, too.

Bright Leaf was a movie about tobacco, and Coop had this great line for me. I was playing a kind of madam, or ex-madam, who was in love with him. I guess I was kind of young to be playing an ex-madam, but what the hell! I suppose I had become respectable. So, Gary came to me to borrow some money, telling me about tobacco. "Sonya," he said, "a man with guts and a workable cigarette machine can make this valley belch fire!" He had to say this with a straight face, and I had to keep a straight face while he said it to me. I was in love with him, and he was in love with Patricia Neal, who was his rich wife who treated him like dirt. He had come crawling back to me, and I told him off, but then I relented. *Bright Leaf* was a period piece, and it would seem funny now, I guess. I'm really not the period type, but it was fun to do. We had Michael Curtiz as the director, too, and he was no slouch.

Geraldine Fitzgerald

I made a picture called *Ten North Frederick* with Gary Cooper in 1958, and it was quite a good film, too, based on a novel by John O'Hara. Gary played a man who could have been President, and I played his terrible wife. He was a wonderful actor, and like Alan Ladd had no idea how good he was. He was very modest, and so self-effacing.

There was one scene in which he was supposed to have a terrible row with his wife, but he couldn't play it, or wouldn't, because he hated that kind of scene. He hated that kind of behavior, too, since he hated to show too much of himself. All of his successful films were tailored for him so that he would never have to do that kind of thing. In that sense he was entirely right about himself, that he should just be the way he was, kind of a god. He was very good with low-key, understated roles, which allowed the audience to feel feelings that Gary himself didn't feel, and to imagine words that he didn't say.

I never found Gary to be anything but genuine. He died not long after *Ten North Frederick* came out, and I remember that he was terribly upset because some reviewer had said that he was too old to play Audrey Hepburn's lover in *Love in the Afternoon*. That hurt him deeply, and I don't think he ever got over it. I can recall saying to him that there was no sign of age on him, and that it wouldn't matter anyway, but that review gave him quite a jolt, and he never recovered. You know, actors and directors and all artists can be terribly injured by ugly reviews. Some of them can't take it, while others start hitting everyone. I know that whatever you do, whether you fight back or refuse to cooperate or act wounded, it is a defense mechanism, because we are all sensitive.

Scene Seven

Dessert

THE FINAL SCENE OF THE PLAY, course of the meal, and chapter of the book is set in W. R. Hearst's spectacular indoor Roman swimming pool. Built entirely of white marble, adorned with colossal classical statues, and glistening with gold-leaf mosaics, it is surrounded by arched windows, through which the full moon is creating a surrealistically beautiful dreamworld from Ravenna.

The selection of desserts is encyclopedic, so the guests look a lot at, but eat only a little of, the rich sweets arranged along a twenty-foot banquet table designed to resemble a gondola. While no one is eager to take a dip, all are more than ready to recline upon the amply cushioned chaise longues that have been wheeled into position. As there is still no sign of Mr. Hearst, Jimmy Stewart resumes his leading role and mentions a piece of advice that Spencer Tracy gave him at the start of his film career.

Bette Davis and Katharine Hepburn both have a few things to say about the great actor, as does Robert Stack, who enjoyed a close relationship with him. It is Loretta Young, though, who contrasts Tracy's discretion and desire for privacy with the flamboyance of Errol Flynn, which prompts Olivia de Havilland to recall the pictures she made with the swashbuckler. Doug Fairbanks reveals his secret role in establishing Flynn's career, and the mention of Fairbanks Sr. leads Katharine Hepburn to extol the silent era as the true golden age of the silver screen.

231

Lillian Gish, First Lady of the American Screen, holds court as she conducts the conversational flow from Mary Pickford and D. W. Griffith to Rudolph Valentino, with all of whom she worked closely. Thus, it is only fitting that the actress who started out as a silent star and then lasted for forty years in the age of sound, Joan Crawford, should be the final subject of scrutiny by Joan Fontaine, Bette Davis, and their friends in this evening odyssey through Hollywood Royalty.

James Stewart

Spencer Tracy once told me something very important about being a Hollywood actor. We were making *The Murder Man*, my first picture, back in 1935, and he said to me, "Don't worry if people come up to you and tell you that you are just playing yourself, that you're not acting. When they come after me and tell me that I'm not acting, that I'm just playing Spencer Tracy, I reply, 'Well, who do you want me to play— Bogey?' " I kind of like the idea of getting up there and playing yourself. After all, they hired us because we had something innate that they wanted. I think it was Laurence Olivier who had the best answer to all this. He said, "I play myself, with deference to the character." Now he was a fellow who was around quite a while, and he was pretty good, too.

The studios sent scouts and casting directors to New York in those days to pick out new faces that would work on film, and I got to know the casting director of this picture. Bill Grady, who was a casting director at MGM, had seen me on stage, I think in Sidney Kingsley's *Yellow Jack* on Broadway in 1934, and he wanted me for a screen test. Here again it's an instance of the little pieces of good fortune that have followed me throughout my life. As I said, you were simply handed a part, and it wasn't a question of their saying, "Do you like it?"—it was your job. So, Grady had been given a script that I was to do, and he told me that shooting started the next week, that I had to get my wardrobe straightened out, and that I had to learn my lines.

Spencer Tracy, ca. 1932

Then he took me up to meet the producer, who said to Bill, "Now, what part do you want this young man to play?" Well, Bill replied that he wanted me to play Shorty. The producer didn't know if it was a joke or not. "What do you mean? You bring me this string bean over six feet tall, nearly seven feet tall, and you want him for Shorty?" the producer shouted. Bill responded that he thought the name of the character could be changed. Well, the producer became indignant, and yelled, "So, you think you can rewrite the script, do you?"

Well, this is the way things happen. I played the part of Shorty without a word of input, and Tracy couldn't have been more helpful. I don't know how many years he had been in the movies, but once again it was the studio system that I have to thank for this great break, getting my first film role in the company of Spencer Tracy, who had had years of training on the stage before he ever came out to Hollywood. The kindness he showed me was unbelievable. He even made an effort to quiet me down, without ever taking me off and actually advising me how to portray this character.

I could see that he was making a great effort to help me, yet never did he make me feel uncomfortable about it. He tried to get me to feel at ease in doing it my way, to give me the idea that I should not get worried about how I would do the lines or how I would act, since I had been signed by MGM to do it naturally, as myself. This was wonderful guidance from a man everyone respected as among the greatest actors in Hollywood. This is probably the first example of the type of help and inspiration I received throughout my career. The really big stars at MGM wanted to help the newcomers, because they knew that the better the final result of a film was, the better it was for them.

Bette Davis

I made *20,000 Years in Sing Sing* with Spencer Tracy back in 1933, but I had only about a three-minute scene in that one. I would have given anything to have costarred with Spencer

Tracy—or Jimmy Cagney, for that matter. They were both wonderful. But Tracy was at Metro, and I was at Warners, and back in the thirties they kept you at your studio most of the time. Much later on, after both of us had made it, we should have done a picture together. But loan-outs were very rare back then, as a matter of fact.

It was very hard for me to get the part in *Of Human Bondage* the following year, for example. It took months of pleading before I ever got the part, and the real reason I got that part was that nobody else would play it. Mildred was a complete bitch, just an horrific character. But I had a great book by Somerset Maugham to read, and it was like a textbook for me to create the role. As an unknown actress I would never have gotten to play her if anyone else had wanted to. Not a single one of the great leading ladies of the day would do it, not one of them, because Mildred was just a total horror.

It was my big chance, an enormous opportunity, which is quite ironic, for it would have been a risk for a major star to play her. But I could only gain by getting the part. I begged Mr. Warner for months on end, and finally he just got sick of hearing me plead, so he agreed to let me do it in order to get rid of me. After I did it and came back to the studio he said, "Well, you see? RKO found out what she was really like, so they sent her back to us!"

That was the first time I worked with Leslie Howard, and then I did two more films with him, *The Petrified Forest* and *It's Love I'm After*. When he became a very well-known actor, his appeal to the women was that he appeared to be so sensitive. Actually, he hated films, and he just laughed at them, which infuriated me, because I loved them. I would say to him that I felt it was too bad that someone who loved them wasn't doing the great parts he was being given. I believe firmly that if you are doing something you should go ahead and do it to the best of your ability. I think you should not beef about what you have decided to do, as he did. He used to read a book off-scene for me while we were shooting *Bondage*.

In fact, the whole English cast was just horrified that an

American girl had been given this part of a British girl. I guess that is understandable, though, that they wanted one of their own to portray Mildred, so that was not much fun for me in the beginning of the filming. I could *feel* how they resented my being cast in the part, and that they felt I was not going to be right for it. But it proved to be the turning point in my career.

As for Leslie, it seemed that every woman in America wanted to mother him, to take care of him. I don't know that he was really so soft and sensitive, but that was definitely his appeal, and the way people felt about him.

Joan Fontaine

When Katharine Hepburn worked with Spencer Tracy it was a special, mutual kind of thing. So there was no need for dramatic power displays.

Katharine Hepburn

Spencer was a brilliant actor, and I learned an awful lot from him. He never overdid it, and he had a remarkable memory, remarkable concentration, so that whatever he said came off a very firm foundation, and with the utmost simplicity. His whole body and mind was back of it, but in a very relaxed way. I think that he and Laurette Taylor were the best actors I've ever seen. She had that same gift, and yet life for them was extremely difficult. Acting was no problem; it was a relaxation. Living was a problem. Acting was their easy chair. They seemed almost alike in many ways.

When Spencer came to New York to do the Bob Sherwood play *The Rugged Path*, in about 1946, Laurette came by the theater and brought a little flower wrapped in a piece of paper. He didn't know her, but he was so thrilled. I was sitting at the top of the balcony of the Plymouth Theatre, which was off-limits, and I could see that he was wearing her flower in his buttonhole, and that he felt comforted. He was on occasion rather uneasy onstage, but that night he was very easy.

Spencer let his personality and character come through his roles, and he made them his own. There was nothing fancy about it. Now, there's something much fancier about me. Is it mannered, or what the hell is it? Lord, is it tricky? I think that Spencer's and Laurette's form of acting was more honorable, more to be admired. The great school of acting, I think, is the baked-potato school, the Spencer and Laurette school.

I made many wonderful films with Spencer Tracy. We started with *Woman of the Year* in 1942, which George Stevens directed, and I thought that one was damned good. We did three with George Cukor—*Keeper of the Flame, Adam's Rib*, and *Pat and Mike*—and we even did one with Frank Capra, called *State of the Union*. The last one was in 1957, *Desk Set*. But you know, the secret to making all of those comedies funny was not the writing or even the acting, but the directing.

It was George Stevens whose wonderful sense of timing made *Woman of the Year* work. He had an almost scientific knowledge of comedy, and he knew how to make them magical. For example, in 1945, when we were working on *Without Love*, in which I played a Washington heiress, and Spencer a scientist who came to live in my house, we had a scene in which Spence was supposed to sleepwalk, and then end up in my bed, and I was supposed to jump out. We rehearsed it and shot it, but it didn't feel right. So I went to see George Stevens about it—and he was not the director of that one. He realized that it wasn't funny because a woman jumping out of bed in that situation isn't funny; it's expected, I guess, if a strange man comes and suddenly climbs into bed with her. So we reversed it to make it ring true. While Spence was sleepwalking I got out of bed to get a hot-water bottle, and he got into my bed, and when I returned with the hot-water bottle, he jumped out, which worked. Working with George Stevens was fascinating, like a course in the ABCs of comedy direction.

Then much later Spence and I made *Guess Who's Coming*

to Dinner, and that was his last film. He died about three weeks after we finished it. It was Stanley Kramer who really persuaded him to do it. He didn't feel too well, but Stanley said, "Well, Spence, are you just going to sit there in your rocker and wait for oblivion?" Stanley couldn't get Spence insured, so he took a big risk in starting that picture. He's a real gambler, but it paid off. He lived up to every single promise he made to Spencer—shooting it all in Hollywood, letting him go home or stay on the set whenever he wanted. Spencer enjoyed it enormously. It was a brilliant script, and Willy Rose will always remain one of the great screenwriters. I won the Oscar for it, but I accepted it for Spencer, too. He deserved it more than I did.

Robert Stack

I used to play polo with Spencer Tracy, and I knew him long before I had any ambitions to become an actor. When I told him that I was going to try to become one he said, "Holy Jesus, we're going to lose a good polo player and wind up with a lousy actor!"

That was back in 1939, and I had walked onto a set by accident, and a fellow said to me, "How would you like to be in pictures?" I said, "Sure, why not?" and that was how I got into the movies. I played Prince Charming, and Deanna Durbin played Cinderella, and I kissed her, the first guy to kiss America's sweetheart on the screen. I had to take a screen test, and I guess I didn't do anything terrible in it, so I got the part in *First Love*. It was an allegory of sorts, I'd say. I was far from pure myself, but at least I had never been caught, so Louella Parsons approved of my presence in the film.

I asked Tracy about it—how I should prepare for the role, if he thought I was ready for the part. He was amazed, and asked me, "You mean they've offered you the lead opposite Deanna Durbin and you think you want to go back East to learn your craft before you try the part? Are you crazy? If you go away and get ready then they'll never be ready for you! Take the part and run with it!" That's what I did, too.

"Opportunity, that's the name of this game," Tracy told me. "Do the best you can, but don't let them rush you. You can go learn acting and do the entire Shakespeare canon to prepare yourself, but when you get back that opportunity may never come again," he said. I never asked him what he meant by telling them not to rush me. I don't know if he meant thinking, or speaking, or what. Of course, I will never be able to ask him now, but in seeing so many of his films I think it was the style of coming across so naturally that he was advising. It served him well, and it appealed to me, too.

As for *First Love*, though, the studio was scared to death that America's sweetheart would suddenly grow up and mature into a woman, and cost them money. I guess that was true of Shirley Temple as well.

There is a kind of nifty story about Spence and me playing polo, and in fact I have a photo of it, with the two of us riding the ponies at the Riviera Field. I later discovered that he had the same picture of the two of us riding together on his dressing room table. My duplicate was kind of feathered around the edges, so I took a pair of scissors and trimmed it down, then called up Tracy's brother and asked if he thought Spence could autograph it for me. He said he thought so, and he said that he would take it to him. At that time Spence had had his first heart attack, but on Christmas Eve I got a wire that said, "Dear Bob, Sorry I can't do justice to the autograph right now, but I will as soon as I can. Merry Christmas, Spence." He couldn't write after having his first heart attack, but can you imagine the courtesy, the class to send a telegram apologizing for not being able to sign a picture? He was such a gent, a true class act. I keep the picture in my trophy room, and you have to use a magnifying glass to read the autograph, which says "To Bob from Spence," but he did it.

Loretta Young

Spencer Tracy was just a darling, and I so enjoyed making *A Man's Castle* with him in 1933. He was stage trained, and he had that ease and naturalness you can get only from experience on the live stage. Most motion picture people had to learn that later on. As a result, Spence was much more in charge of his performance than I was. I think I learned a great deal from him acting-wise, because you simply couldn't help but act with him, he was so easy. He was a very warm, charming, appealing man, I might add.

He was separated from his first wife when I met him, and he used to talk about his son John, who was deaf. The way he talked about his son was so sensitive, but not maudlin at all. It was so loving, I would have to say. I'm sure there have been many women who were crazy about Spencer. He made women feel warm and wanted, but there was no flattery about him. You believed him when he told you something, even though it was something you wanted to hear. There was an honesty about him that was even more complimentary than someone just palavering over you. He never would do that.

There were so many wonderful men in my life back then. Spencer Tracy and Clark Gable and Cary Grant all had an innate elegance about them, which I found so appealing. They were all very private people, and I liked that. In the case of someone like Errol Flynn, for example, I have always felt that there was an awful lot of talk about nothing. I never knew Errol, and I have nothing on which to base that statement, but it seemed to me that he was rather bawdy with his life.

Gina Lollobrigida

I made *Crossed Swords* with Errol Flynn in 1954, and what I remember is that we were playing a love scene, filming a kiss, and in the middle of it he got sick. He took ill right in my arms, and had to stop. He was so yellow with jaundice, from all that drinking, that he had to leave the set for one month. When he returned we finished the kiss scene, but I will never forget that when he started the kiss he looked healthy, and when he finished kissing me he was so skinny and yellow. He was also a lot of fun to be with. Once he tried to show me how

Bette Davis and Errol Flynn, *The Sisters*, 1938

to make vodka with a potato in the bathroom, but I could never figure it out.

Bette Davis

I did *Elizabeth and Essex* with Errol in 1939, as well as *The Sisters* the year before, in which he was very good indeed. He played a straight part for a change in that one, and I've got to say that he was excellent. He would never allow anyone to call him an actor, however, for he had no ambitions in that direction. He thought that anyone who cared about doing a good job or who worked very hard at it was ridiculous. He thought that I was absurd. Whatever he thought of working in the movies, though, he was probably one of the handsomest men ever photographed. There is no question about that. He was just *beautiful*. But he refused to work very hard.

Olivia de Havilland

Bette and I were up for a lot of the same roles, and in fact she tested for the part I played in *Captain Blood*. That role would not have been native to her, though, since it was sort of a romantic heroine part. Bette was a year older than Errol, too, so it would have been a better choice to pick someone younger, as I was, by seven years.

Oh, Errol had such magnetism! There was nobody who did what he did better than he did it. He cared a great deal about his work. He was much more than a swashbuckler. Oddly enough, I never got to know him very well, even though we made seven films together. In those days, if you were a girl, and you were attracted by somebody, as I was by him, you did not let the other person know. It was unthinkable! And there were all these rumors about his seeing Lili Damita anyway. On the set of *Captain Blood* one day an English girl showed up, brown-haired and brown-eyed, and he had been engaged to her. We got along nicely, but then she went back to England, so he finally married Lili.

He never guessed that I had a crush on him. And it didn't get better, either. In fact, I read in something that he wrote that he was in love with me when we made *The Charge of the Light Brigade* the next year, in 1936. I was amazed to read that, for it never occurred to me that he was smitten with me, too, even though we did all those pictures together. It would have been most improper, because he was married to Lili, so it was just unthinkable. Anyway, she went off to Morocco for about four months, so they were obviously separated, and this was back in 1935, when *Captain Blood* came out. I really don't understand their marriage, for she had a tremendous psychological hold over him. It was a powerful relationship, but I'm not sure it was a loving one, though of course it was a sexual one. She was an elegant and bewitching woman who belonged to the international set, and she had great glamour, there's no question about that. She moved in very attractive circles, so that could have had some power over Errol.

I know that there have been suggestions that in addition to his activity as Don Juan he also liked the boys, but I don't believe that for a minute. I think that rumor was started by Tyrone Power's wife, Linda Christian. My theory is that she did all this for pure mischievousness, perhaps because Tyrone and Errol may have teased her, but I don't believe that Errol and Tyrone were lovers. There have been many lies written about Errol—about his involvement with the IRA, about his foul language. I never heard bad language come out of his mouth ever. I suppose it might have with the fellows, but I *never* heard it.

Dodge City was my fourth picture with Errol, and I wasn't a bit happy making that one, and it got pretty dreary, for I had gotten to the point that I did not want to be just "that leading lady for him" anymore. I was eager to do something infinitely more complex and difficult. I was really more than ready, and had been for quite a long time, so *Dodge City* was a discouraging experience for me.

My most vivid memory of *Santa Fe Trail* involves Ronald Reagan, who had the second lead, after Errol. Ronnie was so affable and nice, and he always seemed to have a sense of responsibility toward the cast, because we shot very late at night out on location. Our hours were determined by two things: sunlight, which had to have gone, since it had to be night, and Errol, since he was often late getting to the set. That meant that our hours were often terribly late, since he could never get there on time. Ronnie felt this rather keenly for the rest of the company, and tried to persuade Errol to be more prompt, so that we would be ready to shoot at the very instant it was dark enough to have the effect of night. He wasn't very successful, I'm afraid, so one night he came over to me and said, "Olivia, I've tried my best, but I'm getting nowhere with Errol. I think we can still arrange things satisfactorily, though, so would you please appeal to him?"

Well, I went into Errol's tent, and he was in uniform, and I explained that Ronald Reagan had come to me to ask me on behalf of the rest of the company to ask Errol to try to arrive on the set earlier in the evening so we could get started shooting earlier and go home before sunrise. Well, Errol was quite upset by my request, and he said, "Why do you have to put it on a personal basis?" I didn't know what that meant, and I was so confused, and terribly hurt, and I said that I didn't know how else to put it. My shock was so great, for I thought of his reply as a kind of reproach and rebuff, which was hard to take. I didn't understand why he said what he did, and I cannot even remember if my mission was successful.

I do remember that I worked with Ronnie later, when he was president of the Screen Actors Guild, and I was on the board of directors. He was really a marvelous chairman, very skillful and adroit, and he made those meetings interesting enough, and attractive enough, so that there was very good attendance. In fact, we kind of looked forward to those meetings, which was remarkable in itself, since they were business meetings of an executive board. It was all because of him. A union is not all that entertaining, but he made those sessions worthwhile. I think that he has always had a sense of public responsibility, and was always a politician without really understanding it. Look how he came to me that time to represent the cast and crew in talking to Errol Flynn. He had that gift, for he certainly kept those meetings alive and to the point. He was always fair, and he never lost his poise, and I've got to say that he was very impressive in that role. That capacity is very special.

I remember *They Died With Their Boots On* very happily. They wanted to rewrite my part to make it more interesting for me, and Errol didn't object, which surprised me, but he didn't feel threatened. It was a good experience, except for that last scene, when they say good-bye, for I had an awful sense of personal grief, when Custer heads off for his death. It was terribly strange, and overwhelming. I thought about it a lot many years later, and then suddenly the answer came to me. It was some kind of personal intuition that we would never work together again.

That was the last film that Errol Flynn and I made together, and subconsciously I knew it. We were in the same film seven different times. Our destinies were so intertwined, and he meant a great deal to me. And he still does. I still enjoy watching him and hearing his voice. Once someone sent me a little cassette as a personal message, so I had an hour, and I thought it would be a good time to listen to it. Well, I put this cassette on, and it had "Pomp and Circumstance" playing in the background. Then it switched to a talking introduction, which said it was going to play a movie theme from another era, which still spoke to a lot of people. It was the love scene from *Robin Hood*, and there was Errol, saying, "You do love me, don't you?" I just could hardly . . . It was terribly affecting after all these years, gone since 1959, and *Robin Hood* was my favorite film with him.

This friend meant very well by sending me the cassette, but it was extraordinary how it affected me, for Errol was a central figure in my life. It was a kind of unreal attachment, after all, for all of these feelings were unfulfilled, but very powerful, just the same. These were two lives, and two careers, curiously meshed as well. Though we never lived our lives together, we lived an important part of our lives together. It was kind of an adolescent romance, I guess, but that doesn't mean it wasn't important. I still think of him with immense tenderness.

Douglas Fairbanks, Jr.

I remember making a film called *Mimi* in London for Warners in 1935 with Gertrude Lawrence, and one of the bit players was Errol Flynn. I was asked to look at his test, which I thought very good, for he had been going to drama school. Warners wanted me to remake some of my father's films, but I objected, feeling that it would be a rank imitation, and told them that if I wanted to do *The Thief of Baghdad* or *The Mark of Zorro* or *Robin Hood* I would do it *my* way. I felt that it would be sacrilege to copy my father's kind of silent picture action. They were being very difficult about it, so I wrote a letter to Jack Warner recommending this young fellow I'd seen named Errol Flynn.

Errol went out to Hollywood as a result of that letter, and contrary to opinion he did not work for Warner first, but started elsewhere, working his way up until he got to do *Captain Blood* in a style very similar to my father's. He had been cast in a small part in it, but the leading man, Robert Donat, fell ill, so they gave him the break he needed, and his career was made. They had already shot half the picture, and Errol had done so well in his little part that they finished filming it with him in the title role. Errol did his end of the bargain very well, but I don't think that Warners did theirs nearly as well.

I never ran around with Errol, but I did know him quite well. We played tennis now and then, and I was with him a lot just before he hit the jackpot. He liked to call himself an amiable scoundrel, and it amused him to build up his reputation like that. He enjoyed having a bad reputation, and he was often badly behaved. I would not like to have been his producer, for he was awfully difficult and irresponsible, laughing at people who were conscientious about their jobs.

He and David Niven were very close, and they got along famously until the war broke out. They did have a bit of a falling-out then, when Niven went off to fight. That rumor about Flynn being a Nazi spy is nonsense, too, for he didn't know enough about what the Nazis were about to have an opinion. In California everyone was so insulated that the war was little more than a rude interruption.

I personally don't think Errol's films were nearly as good as my father's swashbuckling movies, since they were manufactured, rather than created by inspiration, as I think my father's best films of the twenties were. That's why I didn't want to do those Warner remakes of United Artists classics from the silent era.

Katharine Hepburn

I still think that the silent era was the golden age of Hollywood, for they made the most beautiful films, and the stars were lovely, and they had such character and personality. They demonstrated honorable qualities by which to live. I guess I'm part of the last generation that grew up instilled with a proper code of behavior. I came of age during a period when people "kept house," so to speak. They don't do it any longer. They keep the television in the living room, and it's just a garbage box, and so if you keep the garbage in the living room it will smell, and you will begin to smell like it.

You know, once I made a trip with Mary Pickford from Los Angeles to Paris, and what a fascinating character she was! I went over and asked her if I could sit next to her, and she said I could, and then I asked if she would tell me the story of her life. And she did. And it was absolutely fascinating, and I was so stupid not to take notes. You know, when you meet someone like that you are so awed and impressed and excited that what they tell you is rather vague in recollection. She told me fascinating stories about that era. The only one we still have like that is Lillian Gish, who is also remarkable.

Lillian Gish

Mary Pickford was from Toronto originally, but her real name was Gladys Smith. The people from Canada always spoke English much better than we did in America, so Mother said that Dorothy and I should listen to the way they pronounced the language, which we did, learning the difference between good and bad English.

Gladys and her sister and her brother were all older than Dorothy and I, and the sister especially had a beautiful face. But she had a mature body, so they had to cover her up so that she could play children in the movies. The Smiths were great friends, and they helped us a lot. Later we wondered what had happened to the Smiths, why they had left the stage to go into the movies, which seemed such a step down. We thought that some terrible hardship had hit them to cause such a lowering of their professional standards, for all three Smith children were child actors like Dorothy and myself. We found to our surprise that they were making much more money than we were, and that they even had an automobile. Well, that was way beyond our thoughts and dreams at that time, back in 1912. An automobile seemed like the ultimate luxury, which we could never have afforded.

One day Gladys introduced us to a man we thought was Mr. Biograph, the name of the company that was making the flickers, as they were called. He was the boss of the Biograph Studio, and, of course, it was Mr. David Wark Griffith. When we met he said to himself, "Gish? Hmmm, sounds like Fish or Pish or Mish. That's a terrible name!" Well, Dorothy piped up to him with "If it was good enough for Mother then it's good enough for us!" After that he never asked us to change our name.

Lillian Gish, *Romola*, 1924

That very day he took Dorothy and me upstairs to rehearse us for a new film, *An Unseen Enemy*. It was about two
children, orphans, who are about to be robbed by an evil
servant. Mr. Griffith couldn't tell the two of us apart, so he
put a red ribbon in Dorothy's hair and a blue one in mine, and
he called us "Red" and "Blue." We made that picture in one
day, and we were paid five dollars each for our work.

Well, we were used to playing for audiences, and for one
day in the theater we would get five dollars, so we thought
that we would get much more for making a movie, but that
was it. Five dollars was worth a lot more then than it is today,
but even so we expected to get a lot more for making a film.
Mother would get five dollars a day for her work, too, so with
all three of us working for Mr. Griffith, we would make
fifteen dollars a day, and that was much more than we had
ever made before.

After Mary Pickford moved to Hollywood and lived at
Pickfair with Douglas Fairbanks, we would visit them frequently. Douglas had built this huge house on the top of a
mountain, so when we were riding up to it he had to sit in the
front seat with a gun, to shoot at the coyotes whenever he saw
one in the middle of the road. There were no other houses
around there at the time, and since he didn't want to kill the
coyotes with the car he would fire the rifle to scare them out of
the way. That's Beverly Hills for you!

Douglas Fairbanks, Jr.

Mary Pickford was my stepmother, and she made *The New
York Hat* with D. W. Griffith in about 1912, when I was just a
tot. Mary Pickford was an absolute dream to me, and we were
very close. What an enchanting, wonderful woman! She was
also a very shrewd, wise woman, and the brains behind
United Artists. It was as much her idea to found that company
as anyone's. I wouldn't say that she exactly dominated the

partnership, but she was definitely a major voice in it, always closely listened to by my father and Griffith.

Lillian Gish

The most incredible thing about Griffith was that he never had a script, in all the time that I was with him. I made a lot of pictures with him, and three of the biggest were *Judith of Bethulia*, *The Birth of a Nation*, and *Intolerance*, all done between 1914 and 1916.

He would rehearse all of the actors in the different parts, depending upon who was available on a given day of shooting, and he had me try the leading role in *The Birth of a Nation*. Then he told me that he was going to film the scene. Well, I had thought that Blanche Sweet was going to play that part. The first time I had any idea that he wanted me for it was when he told me to go and get measured for the costumes. All I could think of was "Why me? Blanche won't like this!"

She had just played the leading role in *Judith of Bethulia*, which was about the ancient Israelites at war with the Assyrians, and I was very surprised to learn that I was to have the big role in *Birth*, which was about the forming of the Ku Klux Klan after the Civil War. But I had a face that could be photographed at any angle. Griffith used to say, "You can photograph her upside down, because it's all even." That's really why I got the parts I did. For instance, Mary Pickford had a side of her face that was like a child's, and the other side was that of a businesswoman's. So she always had a certain angle from which she demanded to be photographed. I always looked the same, and that is the real reason that I got so many of the roles I did.

I think that Mr. Griffith was in love with my mother, too. He was her age, and once when he went away he asked Mother if she had a safe-deposit box. She said that she didn't, so he told her to get one, to charge it to him, and to keep a big package wrapped up in newspapers for him. He was heading for Europe, and told her not to look at what he was entrusting her with.

So, that's what she did, and when he returned she gave the package back to him, and he said to her, since he could see that she hadn't opened it, "This is all the money I have in the world." She knew then how much he trusted her, even though he had a family of his own elsewhere. His own brother was working with him in the film business, but he trusted Mother more than any of them, and I think it was because he loved her.

He wasn't a businessman at all. He was a poet at heart. If he sold a poem he had written for ten dollars it made him happier than any big picture he ever directed. He had no sense at all for money. He was destroyed by the film business, even though he gave the motion picture medium its form and its grammar.

He went into the film business in 1908. It was about five years later when we met him, and about five years after that when Dorothy discovered Rudolph Valentino. She had been out one evening dancing, and there was this man out on the floor, dancing with the ladies. One member of Dorothy's party knew him and brought him over to the table, where she asked him if he would be interested in getting into the movies. He immediately said that he would be very interested, so the next day she told Mr. Griffith about Valentino. She said that she had found a man whom all the women would like, photogenic and romantic looking. But when Valentino came in Mr. Griffith told him that he thought he wasn't quite right. "I don't think the girls will like him, because he's too foreign looking," Griffith told me. So, Mr. Griffith didn't hire him, but Valentino went on to become one of the biggest stars of all time, and the women went crazy for him. Dorothy was right, for she had a better eye for actors than Griffith did.

Rudolph Valentino was a very shy man, but he would come to our house and cook dinner for us, usually spaghetti. The idea of being in the movies scared him, but Mother took an interest in him and tried to help him. He was a terribly nice man, but he died early, and that was from embarrassment. He just couldn't take it all, with the constant attention and exposure and invasion of privacy. It killed him.

Loretta Young

I was an extra on *The Sheik* back in 1921, and I just loved being in "the flickers," as we called them. Valentino was so young and attractive, too.

They would get us up at five in the morning, where we were all living in tents out in Ventura, and after the bells would ring to wake us up they would take us over to these big tin tubs. We would stand in the middle of a tub, and they would tell you to hold your nose and close your eyes, and they would pour Bowlamania all over you, to turn us all brown, since we were playing Arab kids. They told us not to rub all the chalky stuff off, to let it dry, and we would shake a little, and then be brown. They would put a rag on your head, send you for breakfast, and then you would go to work. I thought that part of it was marvelous, but I didn't like coming back at night, because they would have to scrub hard to get it off. Then you would have to go through the same thing the next day. Eventually I got to the point that I would just rinse off.

Valentino would come back to the tents at around four-thirty, when it got too dark to film, and he would take us up on that beautiful white horse, one at a time, all ten of us. He did that every single night, and it was such a treat. Valentino was just darling to us.

Douglas Fairbanks, Jr.

Rudolph Valentino and Mary Pickford and Charlie Chaplin and my father were all superstars, and Greta Garbo certainly was. Clark Gable was near to it, as was Katharine Hepburn, but I don't think that there have been *any* superstars since the days of the silent pictures. It's just impossible to be one now,

Rudolph Valentino, ca. 1925

since there is a language barrier. I don't even believe in the term "superstar," which I think is a cliché.

Katharine Hepburn

I think you could say that, because the medium itself really changed when sound came in. There were very few stars who made the transition: Greta Garbo, Norma Shearer, and Joan Crawford, but not many others.

James Stewart

I got to know Joan Crawford when I made *The Gorgeous Hussy* with her in 1936. She was a very considerate and professional actress, and a lady. I had only a very small part in that film, but she was extremely pleasant to me, and to everyone else, as far as I could see. I never saw anything like the behavior described in *Mommie Dearest*, and as far as I know no one else who really knew her did either. She was the star of that picture, which had a splendid cast, including Lionel Barrymore, Robert Taylor, Melvyn Douglas, and Franchot Tone, who was Joan's husband at the time.

Joan Fontaine

I got to know Joan Crawford very well when we were making *The Women* under George Cukor in 1939. There wasn't one bit of trouble among us, and it was a hoot from start to finish, because George was just the most wonderful director, so civilized and tactful, and with such a sense of humor. If anyone had said, "Now look here, you're standing in my camera line," George would have handled it so skillfully that we all would have broken out laughing.

Paulette Goddard was in that one, and she was married to Charlie Chaplin at the time. Rosalind Russell was also in it, and she was a pretty strong lady, and a lady indeed. Because of her height, she had a Charlotte Greenwood complex, I

Joan Fontaine, *Frenchman's Creek*, 1944

think—a kind of angular, palsy, tomboyish, backslapping manner.

Norma Shearer had the lead in *The Women*, and she was simply charming, and Joan Crawford was going through her intellectual phase, wearing horn-rimmed glasses and being so terribly ladylike. She would place the knitting ball at her belly button and knit away, speaking in her dulcet voice, and wearing the first bare midrift gown Adrian ever designed.

Joan was a manufactured personality, totally self-invented, and I think she did a pretty good job of it. She came to my home, and I went to hers, and she wasn't treating her children that way. I won't have it! It wasn't at all like her daughter wrote in *Mommie Dearest*. I recall one night that I went to her home, and all four of the children were there, all four of them adopted. They were in their little dressing gowns, and they said their prayers. I myself would not have had my children say their prayers in front of guests, but I would have brought them in, as she did, to kiss everybody and to say good night, for they looked adorable and perfectly happy.

I remember once at a dinner party at my house we were on dessert, and someone mentioned that it was Mother's Day, and two diamond tears appeared on Miss Crawford's face. "Joan," she said, "you will excuse me, but I must go home." And she left the dining table and drove home. I'm sure that life in Joan Crawford's household was a difficult situation at best, but I saw no evidence that Christina was ever abused. But then that kind of behavior isn't limited to show business. Look at what Elliott Roosevelt did, dragging his family name into the mud. He didn't need the money, so what's the point? Self-disgrace?

Rossano Brazzi

I made a film with Joan Crawford, and it was a very famous book before we filmed it. I know that it was *A Certain Smile* that I made with Joan Fontaine in 1958, and that it was *Light*

Joan Crawford, ca. 1937

in the Piazza that I made with Olivia de Havilland in 1962. What was the name of that picture I did for Columbia with Joan Crawford, though? Ah, it was *The Story of Esther Costello*, and we did it in England in 1957, and in America it was called *The Golden Virgin*. I played a younger man who married Joan for her money, and I was having an affair with her adopted daughter. Joan's daughter was blind, for as a child she had been in a fire, and it was a terrible shock for her. The end of the movie had the two of us driving into a tunnel, where we were killed.

Maybe the trouble with making too many movies is that you can't always recall the titles from thirty years back, much less fifty. In any case, Joan Crawford was fantastic to work with. She was very professional, but perhaps just a little too much so. She actually slept at the Shepperton Studios, where we were making the picture, and she would get up at four in the morning to exercise in the gym for an hour, prior to three hours of makeup and hair. By the time we were ready to shoot at eight-thirty she was already tired, and ready to go back to her bungalow. Nonetheless, she was marvelous to work with, and she remained a good friend.

I remember that she was there in London with Alfred Steele, the head of Pepsi-Cola, who became her husband. Joan was a woman born to work. She cared about nothing except making movies. I recall that I was staying at the Savoy Hotel with my wife, and all the critics in London got together to give Joan a party there. Since I was the leading man in the picture I was invited, too, and of course my wife was to accompany me. But at the last minute my wife had to await a telephone call from Italy, so she stayed in the room. The plan was for Joan, my wife, and me to attend the cocktail party for perhaps an hour, after which we would all go to dinner at some party in her honor, surrounded by all the journalists.

After half an hour, my wife came down to join us, and my wife had a personality that would kill everybody. After ten minutes Joan and I were completely ignored, and all the journalists had crowded around Lydia Brazzi, who really was a captivating lady. Joan disappeared as soon as she saw that she was being upstaged by my wife, who had no intention of doing any such thing, I am sure. Alfred then explained that Joan had a little headache and would not be able to join us for dinner, but Alfred did, and he spent most of the night dancing with Lydia. The next day one hundred roses came for Lydia with a tiny card which said, "Dear Lydia, As a woman I understood it, but as an actress I couldn't take it. Love, Joan." I remember that later, when we were back in Hollywood, Joan would go to the kitchen with my wife to cook on Sunday mornings, too.

Bette Davis

It is simply unbelievable to me that with only one film in common, Joan Crawford and I are talked about as if we were a couple. We did make *What Ever Happened to Baby Jane?* But why, with only that one association, we should be so closely connected in people's memories or imaginations is beyond me. No two more opposite human beings ever lived, I can tell you. I mean that professionally as well as personally.

She was certainly good in *Baby Jane*, for she was on time, and she knew her lines. I mean, she was a pro. But there were no problems during the making of it—to the great disappointment of the press, who couldn't wait to print that we were locked in heated combat, that we were jealous rivals. It simply wasn't like that. One day Miss Crawford suggested that we write on the wall of the studio: "Sorry, everybody, but we're getting along very well." I thought that would have been cute.

Of course she was supposed to do *Hush . . . Hush, Sweet Charlotte* with me, but she said that she was ill, and thus could not do it as planned, so that shut us down for about three months. When it became clear that she was not going to recover, Mr. Aldrich got Miss de Havilland to play the part. She was very good in it, too, I must say.

During the filming of *Dangerous*, though, which I made with Franchot Tone back in 1935, he was courting Miss

Crawford. They would go off to lunch together every day, and he would come back covered in lipstick. He would be very proud of it, too, for vanity's sake. He was actually a good actor, I thought. Franchot Tone came from an elegant sort of family, but his career never really did work out for him the way he wanted, the way it really should have. And I got my first Oscar for that picture, too. But there's no question about it: it was a consolation prize for my work in *Of Human Bondage*. Anyway, Mr. Tone married Joan Crawford later on.

Douglas Fairbanks, Jr.

I was only about nineteen when I married Joan Crawford back in 1928, and I remember only very nice things about her. She was very hardworking, and terribly conscientious, even to the point of people making fun of her, since she was always trying so hard, studying voice and singing even though she did not have a fine singing voice. But she was determined, and wanted to know the technique of it. She devoted herself entirely to whatever she was doing, going into all kinds of preparation for whatever part she was trying to learn.

I have never seen anyone who worked so hard to do her best. She had no sense of humor about it, either. If you told her something was funny she would laugh in a forced way, even though it might have been a terribly amusing joke. She wouldn't really think it was funny, though, because she was just so serious about her work.

I remember that I was appearing in a play in the late twenties, and she came to the opening night, after which she wrote me a fan letter, asking me to give her a ring sometime. We had friends in common, so I did, and that's how we met. She was three years older than I, but everyone thought that I was older than she, since I used to make myself up to look older in order to get jobs. When I was sixteen I would say that I was twenty-one, and they would believe me.

Her real name was Lucille LeSueur, and our marriage lasted about five years, though we were together perhaps only three. That was simply because I, as a young fellow, had one idea about how to live with a wife, and she had a completely different idea. I had an appetite for all kinds of things in life, many of them away from film work, such as traveling and living around the world. Movies simply were not the whole world to me. I worked hard as an actor, but Hollywood just wasn't everything to me. Joan wasn't even interested in the theater. All she cared about was her job at MGM.

When we went abroad, which was her first time out of the country, she absolutely hated every minute of it, and couldn't wait to get back in front of the cameras in Culver City. She was very frank about it, and didn't pretend to feel otherwise. It was like going back to the womb for her, the only place where she felt secure and confident in herself. It was where all of her hopes and ambitions were centered. Her life was right there, and all of her values, too. I was simply not so dedicated to making movies and being a star, and that's what the difference in us was, as well as why our marriage didn't last.

As for the character depicted in *Mommie Dearest*, I'm not sure that what the daughter had to say was so accurate. But then, I didn't know Joan at that point in her life, since we had been divorced for years; and although I would see her in restaurants and say hello we were no longer close. I do know that her secretary was with her for thirty-five years, and she says that she doesn't remember ever seeing anything like that at all.

Now even allowing for loyalty and devotion, and that she might be stretching the truth just a bit, which wouldn't surprise me at all, too many other people knew Joan very well, and none of them ever saw this dominating kind of character described in the book and in the film. When I knew her she didn't drink at all, and she wouldn't even sip wine. My father never had a drink in his life, and Joan and he used to tease each other about being teetotalers. If the booze happened at all, it was much later. And I don't recall ever seeing her in a temper, even though we had disagreements, albeit civilized ones. I surely would remember if we ever had any big rows, but I don't recall one.

Katharine Hepburn

What a disgusting thing for Joan Crawford's daughter to do! What a profound betrayal! And Bette Davis' daughter, too! No matter what the situation, it's family business that should never be discussed. And to sell it is cheap and revolting! Shame, shame, no matter what!

But then it sells, since everyone wants to know about the private life behind the screen image. If it smells, it sells, it seems. It's like watching a street accident. You are horrified and appalled, and yet you simply can't take your eyes off it. A perfectly ghastly state of affairs! Just sensational filth, but then you can't put it down. You can't wait to find out what's around the corner. Well, I'm as culpable as anyone else, I guess.

Things certainly didn't used to be the way they are now, though. Mary Pickford and the others back then led their lives with discretion and restraint. You know, the rules of living with one another have been thrown away. Rules were made for practical reasons, to be easy to follow. But when we give them up, the truth doesn't matter any longer. And so you find yourself believing in nothing.

Personally, I've never found it difficult to tell the difference between right and wrong. But today we are living in an age when anything goes. I don't see how we became so obsessed with money, and with selling. I think all of this emphasis on the commercial value of this or that promotes a dangerous attitude. In my view, we're far too concerned with the material today. And everyone is struggling to be noticed. I think that's one reason for all of this terrorism. You can do almost anything these days and get away with it, so who really knows who is right or wrong any longer? When the truth goes out of style, life become extremely difficult. We just don't know what the truth is any longer, and that goes for everything.

Jack Lemmon, ca. 1964

Rossano Brazzi, ca. 1955

George C. Scott, ca. 1960

Rod Steiger, ca. 1949

Robert Stack, ca. 1956

Afterword

WHILE THE GUESTS MAKE THEIR WAY BACK from the glittering mosaic pool, moving from fifth-century Ravenna to the Florentine Renaissance of the lavishly appointed bungalows where they will spend the night, let us pause a moment to consider how much they, and those they have discussed in these seven chapters, have meant to us all, individually as well as collectively.

As the living icons, the dominant role models of several generations, they have not only influenced fashion and taste, but also established styles and codes of behavior, and perhaps even inspired many through their film personas to struggle on, to try harder, to be better people.

This book might have been entitled *Guess Who Came to Dinner*, and it might have been followed by the sequel *Guess Who Stayed for Breakfast*. In naming it *Hollywood Royalty*, I have sought to honor the two dozen artists who graciously extended to me the courtesy of prolonged interviews, and to acknowledge the pivotal role that they have played in the creation of twentieth-century culture. Without their royal examples, we would all be much the poorer, so let us count ourselves all the richer for the hundreds of classic works of film art that they leave for us and for future generations in need of role models and ideals.

Gregory Speck and Audrey Hepburn, 1992, by Bettina Cirone

ABOUT THE AUTHOR

NOTED BON VIVANT, raconteur, and aesthete Gregory Speck has been widely published—over seven hundred articles in *Interview*, *Us*, *Elle*, *Gente*, *Horizon*, *Stagebill*, the New York *Daily News*, and elsewhere; quoted by top gossip columnists; and globally syndicated—by the *New York Times*. A celebrity interviewer, cultural critic, and high society chronicler who has traveled to over sixty countries, this habitué of Manhattan's fast lane, member of Virginia's landed gentry, and multilingual jet setter is also a prize-winning poet and painter, a classical musician, and an accomplished photographer. A graduate of Woodberry Forest School, Amherst College, Université de la Sorbonne, and New York University, our Renaissance man-about-town is already at work on his next book.